SPIRITUAL WARFARE

By

His Holiness Pope Shenouda III

Spiritual Warfare

By His Holiness Pope Shenouda III
Second Edition, June 2022

First Edition October 1990 Translated by Wedad Abbas and
revised by Dr. Angeile Botros Samaan

Fully revised and edited by:
St. Shenouda Monastery
8419 Putty Rd, Putty, NSW, 2330
Australia

ISBN: 978-0-6451395-7-0

Special thanks to all who helped, God reward you all.

Cover page by Lydia Soliman.

H.H. Pope Shenouda III
117th Pope and Patriarch of Alexandria and the
See of St Mark

CONTENTS

HISTORY OF THIS BOOK

It was necessary to publish a collection of books about spiritual wars, as it is one of the most important topics relating to the life of man. The first book in this series was "Diabolic Wars."

This book is the second in this series. It was originally in the form of lectures during the sixties, with the first article being titled *"The Love of Praise and Honour."* This article was presented at a meeting for the ministers in St. Minas Church in Alexandria,1965. Printed and published by St Mary's church in Moharram Baik, it has since been distributed many times and is also included in this book with a few changes.

The articles were published by the 'Watani' Newspaper" throughout the year 1985 and now we are happy to publish them in a book to make them more accessible.

There are many other topics which we shall publish successively, God willing, under the title of Spiritual Wars. Among these topics, there will be a book dealing with the topic of "Anger" and perhaps another concerning "The sins of the tongue." This subject is also briefly dealt with in this book. Some of the fathers have dealt with this idea of spiritual wars. In their articles, they covered the eight thoughts which fight against the soul. These are gluttony, adultery, wrath, sadness, laziness, lust of possessions, vain glory and pride. However, most of these thoughts were presented in the context of monasticism and can be seen in the works of John Cassian and St Evagrius. I refer you to their writings regarding these topics.

We have tried to include almost all the spiritual wars, their causes, their signs and their remedies in this book.

Until we meet again in the third installment of Spiritual Wars, may God lead you in triumph towards Him (2 Cor. 2:14)

POPE SHENOUDA III

CHAPTER 1

WARS INSIDE AND OUTSIDE YOU

INTRODUCTION

No one's life is void of wars.

Even the lives of the holy fathers were plagued with spiritual wars, some of which were external from the devils and a few internal.

As for diabolic wars, they are explained in another book which I have already published. In it, I deal with 25 kinds of diabolical wars. I have also mentioned eleven methods which can be used to overcome them. As such, I shall give a few hints about them in this chapter.

Among external wars, there are some that can be caused by outer offences. Such offences can come from our environment or bad friendships. I shall deal with these two points here and I also recommend reading about them in my book *Life of Purity and Repentance*.

In dealing with internal wars, I shall concentrate on two main points; thoughts and lusts. Thoughts fight the mind and lusts fight the heart and senses. You will find another chapter in this book about these besides what is included in this chapter.

Spiritual wars may be provoked from within, from the devil, from the world, from wicked people or from other people.

Internal Wars

These wars come from lusts of the heart, thoughts of the mind and motions of the body.

An internal war is more severe than an external one. This is because it is one waged against oneself. It is a hard war because one desires it and refuses to resist it and because of this, purity of the heart is the most important thing in one's life. According to one of the saints, *'A pure heart is an unattainable (impregnable) fortress.'* The heart resembles a house built on rock. Whatever storms blow outside, no harm can be done to it (Matt. 7:24,25).

A person who has no internal wars, if attacked by an external one, finds it light and can overcome it easily. This is because their heart refuses it and their will is not inclined to respond to it or accept it.

An internal war may come from being involved in sin. Here one is fought by past things already implanted in one's heart and mind.

It may also be due to laziness or a weak nature, resulting in submission to sin. Internal wars may be provoked by one's negligence to practice spiritual exercises. This weakens the heart and leaves the mind to go astray without any control. This war may begin when one neglects to control their senses, which in turn allows evil thoughts to enter.

An internal war may either be light or violent. Even though it is light at the beginning, it eventually dominates one who takes it for-granted.
Among internal wars there are:

<u>+ War of thoughts.</u>

Thoughts may come while awake or asleep. During sleep, thoughts may be the product of news and gossip during day. They may also be due to lusts, ideas settled inside the mind, tales heard by others or material that has been read that leave an imprint in the mind. All these come in the form of dreams, wandering of the mind or what is called daydreams. By these a person indulges the thoughts if their heart accepts them. If the heart refuses them, they stop and the person comes to themselves.

One's will is an important restraint for thoughts, as it is the key by which they enter. Even if a thought enters stealthily, a person's will either allows it to remain or stops it.

Hence is the importance of being responsible.

The question is; 'Are those thoughts voluntary, involuntary, or semi-voluntary?' The answer is, they are now involuntary but are a result of a previous willingness.

The devil may plant a thought in one's mind, introducing it without their will. However, despite being responsible for its entry, you are now responsible for accepting it. You can dismiss such a thought if you want and neither argue with it nor welcome it. In case you accept such a sinful thought, you betray the Holy Spirit dwelling within you and betray God's love. You are considered in this case, failing to keep God's commandments and the holiness of your heart.

A sinful thought may come to you in a dream. If you are entirely pure, you will refuse it, even in a dream. However, if you are not at this level and accept it, you will feel much sorrow for it upon wakening. This sorrow will leave a deep impression on your inner mind and this will help you refuse any similar dream in the future. If this does not happen directly, it may happen gradually until you attain the purity of the inner mind.

So, resist the sinful thoughts by day in your wakefulness to be able to resist it by night in your sleep. Such resistance becomes implanted deep within your feelings until your inner mind gets used to it.

You have the control over your thoughts, whether they are created by you, introduced to you by others or the devil himself. This proves the following saying true, *'If you cannot prevent birds from hovering about your head, you can prevent them from making a nest in your hair!'*

With your own will and the work of grace within you, you can overcome thoughts so that they stop having control over you. Thoughts cannot make you lose your purity so long as you do not respond to them. True are the words of St. John Chrysostom who said, *'No one can do harm to a person unless he harms himself.'*

So, do not yield to thoughts. Let everyone be wise, and consider the thought, how it begins, how it develops and how it enters one's mind. Let them know that although a thought may appear innocent and calm, it ultimately has a sinful end. Let everyone be on their guard and give no opportunity to a thought, lest it become more severe.

Even when thoughts press hard and continuously on you, do not be willing to submit to them thinking that there is no point to resist them. Despair makes a person slacken towards a thought, opening their inner gates to them. They get weak and fall. I advise you to fight these thoughts and conquer them.

HOW??

+ How Can You Overcome Thoughts?

1. Do not be afraid of thoughts or think they can overcome you, but say with the Apostle, *"I can do all things through Christ who strengthens me."(Phil.4:13).*

Be firm in fighting thoughts and remember the beautiful words, *'Bringing every thought into captivity to the obedience of Christ..." (2Cor.10:5).*

2. Train yourself to lead your thoughts and do not allow them to lead you.

3. Always fill your mind with spiritual matters, so that when the devil introduces a bad thought, he finds the mind preoccupied and unwilling to welcome it in. As a protective remedy, keep yourself busy.

So, do not leave your mind empty lest the devil should occupy it and implant whatever he wants in it.

Spiritual reading is of great benefit. It not only engages the mind and keeps away bad thoughts, but it also has the advantage of providing the mind with spiritual material for meditation. It also fills the heart with feelings of love for God, giving the mind the power to dismiss contradictory thoughts.

4. Always be alert, watching the purity of your heart lest sinful thoughts should overwhelm you without you realizing it.

Dismiss thoughts from the beginning while they are still weak, and you are still powerful.

If you let sinful thoughts remain in your mind for some time, they will soon settle and take hold of you. As they remain and settle within you, you become weak and unable to resist, eventually falling. So, be watchful and quick in dismissing thoughts and remember the words of the Psalmist;

"O daughter of Babylon, who are to be destroyed. Happy shall he be who takes and dashes your little ones against the rock."
(Psalm 137:8,9).

Here, the Psalmist addresses Babylon, the land of captivity which took his heart captive. He says, '*...happy shall he be who takes your little ones...*' i.e., sins which are still small in their beginning, before developing *"...and dashes them against the rock.".* That rock was Christ (1 Cor.10:4).

5. There is a virtue of the mind known as *'spiritual alertness'.* This means to have your mind attached to God in prayers, contemplation, words of love, praises, and songs. Through this, your mind will begin to shy away from engaging in sinful thoughts because of its connection to God. So, it refuses them, thus becoming a spiritual remedy.

Hence, engaging the mind with God is a protective remedy against sinful thoughts, as an attachment to God makes the mind alert.

6. On the other hand, keep away from offences which may bring you sinful thoughts.

Keep away from any harmful gatherings, any bad friendships, or contacts. Avoid reading any material which may bring you filthy thoughts or lead you astray from spiritual thoughts. Avoid hearing, looking at or talking about such matters and avoid anything which brings wicked thoughts.

7. As senses are the gates of the mind, keep them pure so that they may bring you pure thoughts.

If you are negligent or weak in your senses, fight yourself. Be on guard and let your senses serve you, not resist you. Hence, meditating on pictures of the saints, hearing about them, listening to hymns and liturgies all help. Add to this by being in the church with its aroma of incense, lights, icons and spiritual rites. All these will provide the heart with spiritual thoughts.

8. Beware of doubtful thoughts that are neither good nor evil.

These thoughts often lead to sinful thoughts. Those who have no control over their mind, letting it go astray, helps it to find a sinful matter and become occupied with it. Instead, fill your mind with God's love or with any useful matter, even with your work, your studies, your ministry or your responsibilities to prevent it from being engaged in useless matters.

9. If you are troubled with a thought and cannot overcome it, flee from it.

Even if you are in solitude or seclusion, leave it and keep in contact with others because talk would dismiss a sinful thought.

This is because your mind cannot be engaged in thinking and in talking at the same time.

Know that solitude - spiritual solitude - means to be alone with God. If it becomes solitude spent alone with evil thoughts, then association with others is a better course of action.

10. Seek the help of prayers to dismiss a thought. The priest addresses God in the Divine Liturgy of St Basil, saying, '*Every thought that displeases Your goodness, O God, may it be cast away from us.*'

There is a spiritual rule I would like to tell you about concerning fighting thoughts and it is the next point.

11. Fleeing from thoughts is better than fighting them because even though you may overcome an evil thought which occupies your mind, it will defile you during the process.

Do not deceive yourself and say even out of curiosity, 'I shall see how a thought proceeds and how it ends'! You know very well that such a thought will do you more harm than good; so do not put yourself in a trial when you already know it's result.

Do not think that this thought that is tempting you is easy, no matter how trivial it may seem, saying to yourself "these thoughts are easily overcome and I can expose their weakness". Why should you waste your power in fighting when just expelling them is an option.

Engage your mind with something chaste and pure so that it may give you strength in your spiritual life. This helps to raise your spiritual fervor instead of engaging your mind with conflicts which avail you nothing but harm.

12. Know also that if thoughts continue, they may lead to other thoughts or lusts. In such cases they become more dangerous because they move from mind to heart and turn from thought to actions.

Here, we move to another point.

+ War of Lusts.

There are numerous lusts such as lusts of the flesh, lust of knowledge, lust of authority and positions, lust of revenge, lust of domination, lust of wealth, lust of ownership and lust of dignity and fame.

These lusts transfer the ownership of the heart from God to something else and you will not be able to fulfill the words of the Lord, *"My son, give me your heart…."* *(Prov.23:26).*

The following are some points of advice:

1. If you are attacked by a certain lust, do not continue in it but try to get rid of it and remember the beautiful saying, *'Rejoice not for a lust which you have obtained, but rather for a lust which you have overcome.'*

The thing which pleases a person the most is to overcome his weaknesses. The pleasure of overcoming your weaknesses is deeper and more fulfilling than any pleasure from fulfilling a lust.

2. If you are exhausted from fighting against a certain lustful desire, do not get desperate and think there is no use.

See what the Lord Jesus Christ can do for you, not what you are unable to do.

The Lord Jesus Christ was able to turn the Samaritan woman into an evangelist and Mary Magdalene into a saint.

Never think you are fighting alone, for God works with you with all His grace, just as He worked with others.

3. Remember those who conquered and do not put before you your previous failures and your weak nature.

God loves you just as He has loved those who conquered their lusts and will work within you as He has done with others. Whenever attacks increase, grace will increase, so cleave to God and seek His help.

4. In your lusts, struggle hard with God until the cloud returns over the tabernacle (i.e You gain God's presence).

Do not be ashamed to pray while you are deep in sin and do not do as our father Adam did who escaped from the face of God and hid himself behind the trees! Whenever you fall, cleave more to God so that He may save you, purify you and lead you to repentance. Say to Him, *'O Lord, fight for me. Overcome Your enemies and do not leave me alone.'*

Say also, *'O Lord, though I am defeated by sin, I am still Your son, regarded as Your lost sheep. I am Your son though I dwell in a far country. You will not forsake me, nor will I forsake You though the enemy tries to separate me from You. Despite being far from You, You are still in my heart. I still love You though I sinned against You'.*

If you sinned against the Lord as St. Peter did when he denied the Lord Jesus Christ, blaspheming and cursing saying, '*I do not know the man'*, yet later when he had repented he proclaimed with humility saying, "*Lord, You know that I love You..."* *(John21:17)*.

5. Do not let sin separate you from God's love but open your heart to Him and say, *'0 Lord, be sure that this sin is due to weakness not to hatred or betrayal.'*

6. You must also be sure that God knows your weaknesses and still loves you.

Trust that even when you are in sin, God works to save you, to attract you to Him and to restore you. It is God who sought Adam and saved him without any attempt from Adam to repent.

7. Though you perform sinful acts of lust you need to also do any spiritual work to help reduce their severity and grip over you, providing a balance within your heart.

Be sure that good will grow within your heart little by little until you get rid of the lusts of sin. When you feel the work of the Holy Spirit within you, do not neglect it or proceed in your lusts but work with Him...

8. When you know your weakness, do not expose yourself to wars again.

External Wars

These wars are aroused from well-known sources; either from the devil or from people, whether they are enemies, friends, or family! These wars may also come from the world, from material things or from surrounding environments with all its offences.

+ Wars From The Devil.

Diabolic wars may be slow and extended, or sudden and violent.

We may not be aware of the slow wars through which the devil attracts his victims. He may use a long gradual advance so that the victim is unaware of what is befalling them.

The devil drugs them little by little and reduces their spiritual fervor slowly. This continues and grows until their lives change. They become aware of it only when it is too late.

Perhaps Solomon the wise was fought in this way. Through luxury, pleasure, possessions and many women he fell (1 Kings 11:1-8) and his fall was in his old age!!

As for violent sudden wars, they resemble terrifying apparitions or false visions. Such things are diabolic delusions.

St. Anthony the Great was fought with such wars and he overcame them through humility, discernment and prayers. He defeated the devils, so they flew away ashamed of him.

However, God does not permit that such wars attack everyone, because *"God is faithful, who will not allow you to be tempted beyond what you are able" (1Cor.10:13).*

One of the violent diabolic wars which happened suddenly was the temptation that befell Job the Just (Job:1,2). We notice that it was with God's permission, within certain limits, that allowed Job to experience these trials and it ended in a good and blessed way (Job 42).

Yet, diabolic wars are not all terror and fearful scenes as St. Anthony experienced, or diseases and disasters like those Job endured. There are other wars waged by the devil through his use of thoughts. He throws them into the mind or introduces lusts in the heart.

Such wars are usually weak at the beginning because they do not come from the person but are introduced by an external medium. They remain settled until a person opens the door for them to enter their heart and feelings. At this point, you have allowed sin to win.

Opening your doors to the adversary who wants to destroy God's kingdom, is considered a spiritual treachery.

It is a treachery against the Lord who accepted to enter your house and stay in it while you, with your own will, permit His enemy into your heart to dwell in it instead of God!

It is a treachery against the Lord who purchased you for Himself and loved you to the end. He committed to you His Holy Sacraments and made your heart a temple for His Holy Spirit (1 Cor. 6:19,20). But here you are, responding to the devil and opening your heart to him and accepting his contradictory thoughts!!

Through this treachery, as you refuse the work of Grace within you, the devil gains power over you.

Do not say, by way of excuse, that external wars are hard! You give them power when you submit to them. If you resist, the devil will become weak before you as the Apostle says, *"Resist the devil, and he will flee from you." (James 4:7).*

A strong heart, firm in faith, honest in love for God, can extinguish all the fiery darts of the wicked (Eph 6:16).

When the heart of David became strong with faith, the power of Goliath the Giant seemed feeble to him (1 Sam. 17:26). When the heart of Moses the Prophet grew stronger, the power of Pharaoh and his army diminished before him, and the waves of the Red Sea did not frighten him. As for you, if your heart is strong, you will never become weak before the wars of the devils. On the contrary, you will be comforted by the words of the Holy Spirit speaking through the prophets;

"Who are you, O great mountain? Before Zerubbabel you shall become a plain!" (Zech.4:7).

If we become weak, we give the devil the dignity he does not really deserve. We make him strong against us although to begin with, he is afraid of us.

I think when the chief devil sends one of his assistants to fight a believer, that devil trembles and says, *'How can I fight such a person who is the image of God and the temple of His Holy Spirit? How can I fight such a valiant person who is surrounded by God's angels that are there to save him? How can I get near a son of God putting on the shield of faith and the helmet of salvation (Eph.6).'*

'What shall I do if he crosses me with the sign of the cross? Where shall I escape if he raises his hands in prayer? How ashamed shall I be if he dismisses me saying "Get behind Me satan!"(Mat 16:23)?

To the astonishment of this weak devil, he finds such a person afraid of him. So, he becomes daring and despises such a person!

When the devil is not afraid, he attacks with severity and if not resisted he will eventually shave off the hair of that person as he did for Samson, pulls out his eyes and makes him grind and be mocked by children (Jud. 16:19-21).

So, do not be afraid of the devil or his power over you. Remember you are the image of God.

An example of a well-known diabolic war is mistrusting God. Another war is despair. So, do not be afraid, for such thoughts are not yours; they are external attacks which come against your will.

The devil throws into your mind thoughts which make you doubt God's existence, His love and care. He throws into your mind thoughts against the effectiveness of prayers and the intercession of saints. Then, while you refuse such thoughts and resist them, the devil says, 'How will you be saved while you have such thoughts within you?' This proves that such thoughts are not yours.'

It is merely a war of thoughts not a fall through thoughts. Even if you fall for a few minutes, it is out of weakness, not dishonesty towards God and He will forgive you.

I advise you to refrain from reading material that brings doubts into your mind. Avoid contact with any person or media which provide you with doubtful thoughts. Such thoughts and material are probably weapons the devil uses in fighting you, so be wise.

This leads us to another point.

+ Harmful Friendships.

Such friendships may be harmful for your spirituality, your beliefs, or your mind. They may destroy your faith and spirituality.

The first fall of our mother Eve was the result of an evil friendship with the serpent.

The fall of Ahab the King was due to his wicked wife Jezebel. The fall of Solomon the Wise also was due to his foreign wives.

So, I advise you to choose your friends well, for they can easily influence you.

I advise you also to choose your partners in marriage well, because they will undoubtedly have an influence on your spiritual life, either raising your spirituality or bringing them down. Marriage partners have a more dangerous and deep effect compared to friends, acquaintances, and companions.

A friend may meet you at certain times, but a husband/wife is your partner for life. So, you ought to choose a godly partner from all aspects; social, spiritual, and doctrinal. You must go into the depth and not be satisfied with the outer appearance.

Let us remember in this concern the words of the Holy Bible, *"Evil company corrupts good habits", (1Cor. 15:33)* and also, *"...a man's foes will be those of his own household." (Matt.10:25).*

An example of this is the parents who prevent their children from fasting, from worship, consecration, from church and from congregations. They even encourage their children to adorn themselves and to indulge in various means of entertainment. They do not act as an ideal religious family!

Another example is the ungodly husband who draws his wife with him into perdition, mocking her godliness. Such a husband does not encourage his wife to proceed in spiritual practices but prevents her from being engaged in any ministry. He even does not give her a chance to fast or partake of Holy Communion! Hence the Lord says, *"...he who loves father or mother more than Me is not worthy of Me..." (Matt.10:37).*

A person may not be able to separate themselves from their relatives and from their family, however, they ought to love God more than them and to obey God more than they obey them. They must not sacrifice their spirituality or their beliefs for the sake of their relatives.

One must always remember the words of the Apostle, *"We ought to obey God rather than men." (Acts 5:29).*

No one is dearer than God or more beloved than Him and nothing is more important than your eternity.

However, there are certain relatives you must stay away from-if not by body, then at least by avoiding taking part in their acts, their conversations or in anything wrong they do.

Yet, some may be subject to wrongdoings due to their shyness. Thus, they participate in such faults due to their own bashfulness!

Hence, a spiritual person must know that there are limits to shyness and that there are certain situations which require firmness, a strong personality and seriousness to get away from offences and their causes.

True is the saying, *'Ask about the companion before asking about the way.'* This is because some of your relatives may have a bad influence on you, thereby destroying your soul. Such a person may introduce into your heart and mind certain principles and thoughts that would lead your life astray.

Know that your real relatives are they who brings you closer to God. Your real friends are they who are righteous and sincere, who protect your good name and care for your salvation.

Let us move to another spiritual war- Offences.

+ Offences.

An offence is any external thing which makes you fall, or which introduces a sinful thought, a sinful emotion, or a sinful lust. Offences may come from hearing, seeing, reading or other senses. You must avoid such offences as much as you can and avoid being yourself an offence to others.

Offences may be imposed on you or we may seek them by longing for them.

Those which are imposed upon you are considered external wars. Those which we seek are internal wars and operate by requiring external satisfaction. In this kind both internal and external wars meet. Its condemnation is more severe and escaping it is more difficult.

The Lord was very firm in His divine command to keep away from offences.

The Lord says, *"...and if your right eye offends you, pluck it out and cast it from you....and if your right hand offends you, cut it off and cast it from you." (Matt. 5:29,30).*

Many of the fathers interpret the offence of the right eye as the offence that comes to you from the person most dear to you and the offence of the right hand refers to the person who assists you most.

Thus, one must keep away from those who are dear and beloved if they cause offence. If you keep in contact with them it may lead to the loss of your eternity. At this point, one does not know whether they can withstand it or not.

The point is to keep away from external wars whatever the price is. Do not fall in them with your own will because you pray every day saying, *"Lead us not into temptation, but deliver us from evil." (Matt.6:12).*

There are certain offences which attract a person, so they hovers about them as a moth hovers near a fire until it burns and dies. This happens despite the moth seeing many other moths burnt before him by the fire. It cannot be dissuaded until it burns like the others!

There may be someone who offends you and makes you fall, then they escape and you perish. They may be able to repent while you find it difficult to repent! So try, with all your power and with the work of grace within you, to keep away from offences, thus avoiding external wars as much as you can.

Certain readings are also among the sources of offences and external wars. Reading affects a person's thoughts and feelings and may form his principles and direct his life.

There are readings which are obviously false or misrepresentations and you must avoid these without needing to consult anyone.

Other readings cause doubts or confusion and others arouse sinful feelings and lusts. It is not sufficient for a spiritual person to keep away from harmful readings. They must read material which would deepen their love for God. This can be a protective remedy against external wars.

If a person is fought with the love of knowledge, they must know that not all knowledge is useful. Instead, some knowledge may make them lose their simplicity or purity and change their outlook on things for the worse! As a result, a spiritual person must be careful in choosing the material they read.

One of the problems of reading is that it plants in the mind thoughts that are not easily erased or forgotten. Such thoughts may need an awfully long time to be removed from one's memory.

Among the reasons for external wars is also.

+ The Environment.

By this we mean the general atmosphere around a person. The thoughts in the environment in which they live, its trends, the lifestyle, the prevailing principles, the manner of dealing and the concepts adopted by all or by the majority.

It would be exceedingly difficult for him to live as a stranger in such an environment, adopting spiritual principles which they do not understand.

Thus, the righteous man dwelling in such an environment torments his righteous soul from day to day (2 Pet. 2:8). Or at least he exerts a great effort to keep to his spiritual course of life. He may also find themselves exposed to various wars because of their spiritual course. What should they do then?

If they can change the environment, it would be much better. If not, they must withstand, resist and conquer. God will not forget their loving labour.

Our life is to bear witness of the truth. If not with our tongues, we would do this through our practical life at the very least. The Apostle advises us, *"Be not conformed to this world,..." (Rom.12:2).* A spiritual life needs struggling, patience and firmness.

Let such a person be sure that in the struggle, they do not fight alone but that the Lord's Grace works with them and *"...he that endures to the end shall be saved." (Matt.10:22).*

Spiritual wars are numerous and we must struggle and conquer. How many are the gifts which the Lord has bestowed on those who conquered (Rev. 2-3).

Struggle then to be among those who conquered so that you may not lose your crown which the Lord, the righteous judge, gives you on the day of judgement (2 Tim. 4:8). The Lord gives everyone their own reward according to their own labour (Cor3:8).

CHAPTER 2

WAR OF THE SELF

Danger Of The 'Self'

The self is the oldest and most dangerous enemy that fought humanity. The devil does not fight you as much as you fight yourself. The self is your big problem.

They that overcome themselves from within, can overcome the world and all the devils; Those who are defeated by the self and stand weak before it, can fall into any sin.

If we review the history of sin in the world, we shall find humanity's self-involvement everywhere. A person who overcomes the self within them, is victorious in every spiritual war. As long as the self does not betray such a person or open their doors to the enemies, they do not care about any external enemy. See how true the words of St. John Chrysostom are in this respect, *'None can do harm to a person unless such a person does harm to himself.'*

The real harm is the loss of the heavenly kingdom and the loss of internal peace; both of which do not come to you from outside as long as you are strong within.

Someone may ask, 'Don't offences come from the outside, such as temptation, lusts, or outer attacks?'

The answer is that outer attacks and offences may come but they have no authority over you. Your own will has the authority and you alone have the power to decide!

Do you accept an offence or a temptation or not? Do you withstand an external war or not?

Joseph the Righteous faced a violent external war at the hands of the wife of Potiphar but he did not fall. As he refused sin inside his heart, he refused temptation and overcame the offence.

The devil offers you suggestions but does not force you to carry them out.

The Self And Sin

Thus, falling in sin is due to the self and not to external temptations. These are simply offences that can be accepted or refused by the self.

It is true that long persistence of such temptations may cause weakness of the self within, resulting in the submission to sin in the end.

In this case, the weakness of the self is the direct cause whereas offences are the indirect cause.

The self, that is strong within, can keep away from outer offences so that it is not affected by such temptations, thereby becoming weak before them. Hence, the first Psalm warns us against the way of the wicked and the seat of the scornful. St Paul also says, *"Flee also from youthful lusts…" (2 Tim 2:22).*

Fleeing here demonstrates a pure self which refuses external sinful influence. So, it was good that Joseph the Righteous escaped, not out of weakness but rather because he was strong. His escape was proof of his power that could refuse sin.

A pure person refuses even the sinful thought. It refuses to argue with such a thought. It expels the thought immediately and gives it no chance to settle and ultimately produce self -weakness.

The self is strong here because it closes the doors of the mind and heart in front of every sinful suggestion and from the devils.

So, the Psalmist sings, *"Praise the Lord, O Jerusalem! Praise your God, O Zion! For He has strengthened the bars of your gates and has blessed your children within you."* (Ps.147:12,13).

Solomon also blesses the righteous self which is, *"A garden enclosed, a spring shut up, a fountain sealed"* (Songs. 4:12).

True is the saying. *'You cannot prevent flies from hovering about your head but can prevent them from making a nest inside your hair.'*

Offences are sure to come, but what is your attitude towards them? How far does the self respond to those offences or refuse them?

One day you might hear exciting gossip or news, what will be your response to it? Would you be intrigued Or would you be unmoved and calm? The words which may excite others must not excite you and you must respond to them calmly and wisely.

Here the self is tested with respect to its purity, power and to its maturity.

When a person falls, I cannot say that the whole matter is due to external wars but it is also due to an internal war within the self. If the self has betrayed God and opened the door for external enemies, we cannot excuse it from responsibility.

Here we may ask, 'Is your self a friend or an enemy to you? Is it on your side or against you?' True is the saying of St. Isaac, *'When you are reconciled with your 'self,' heaven and earth will be reconciled with you.'*

This means that if you can reconcile within you, your body, your mind, and your soul, the three may then proceed in one direction, the spiritual path. If you are reconciled with your self, the body will not war against the spirit or the spirit against the body, so then the heavens and earth would be reconciled with you. In this case, you will not sin against God, against people or against yourself ...

Wrong Self-Love

What does it mean to love ones-self? Does it mean to spoil yourself and give it whatever it desires? Does it mean to praise it, glorify it, and favor it?

If you do this or something similar, then your love for yourself is the wrong type of love.

True self-love is to lead it in a spiritual way, attach it to God's love and lead it to His Kingdom.

True self-love is to rebuke that self when it does wrong and to correct its conduct when it deviates, even if you are to punish it or resist its sinful desires.

However, sometimes the self wants to lead a life of pleasure. These could be pleasures of the body, senses or pleasures of the world and its lusts. Here you are fought by your own self and you must resist it with all your power, always remembering the words of the Lord;

"If anyone desires to come after Me, let him deny himself and take up his cross daily and follow Me." (Luke 9:23).

The Lord puts before us self-denial as the main virtue of life with Him, even though this may require a person to take up their cross daily.

Many are those who have wrong self-love. Among the aspects of wrong self-love is magnifying the self.

+ Magnifying The Self.

Sometimes we want ourselves to always be great and magnificent, however this often leads to mistakes being made because we seek the wrong way of achieving it.

One wants oneself to be great externally, leaving the internal person in disarray.

From without means through outer appearances, such as positions and titles, wealth and fame, or praise of people. All such matters have no relation to the nature and purity of the 'self.' Instead, they are against it and show ignorance and lack of understanding. See what the Psalmist says;

"The King's daughter is all glorious within. Though her clothing is woven with gold and in robes of many colours'' (Ps. 45:13,14).

What then is the inner glory? Is it that everyone wants to be spiritually great?

Inner glory is when the self restores the image and likeness of God after which it has been created (Gen. 1:26,27).

Inner glory of the self is to be clothed in the fruits of the Spirit i.e., love, joy, peace, longsuffering, gentleness etc. (Gal. 5:22). It also means to be pure, holy, chaste and blameless in everything, to be humble, calm, compassionate and wise. Such is true glory, and whoever trains themselves in these virtues genuinely loves themselves spiritually.

What spiritual benefit does the self avail if it is praised by others? What is the value of such praise when compared to eternity? Is outer dignity a spiritual means to magnify the self, or is it a spiritual war in which many fall?

Self-worship or self-adoring is a feature of such war.

A person in this case wants to see themselves perfect in their own eyes and in the eyes of others; without blemish or defect. They seem to believe that their self is infallible and can do no wrong.

Such a person has self-admiration, just like a person who always likes to look in a mirror and see their own good points. They cannot endure an insult however small it may be, cannot endure criticism and cannot endure any frank opinion contrary to themselves. They think that all this spoils their image while they want it to remain perfect in the eyes of people. Since such a person does not accept a frank opinion or criticism they do not remedy their faults and don't correct their conduct or change their character. Thus, self-love leads them away from internal purity. Hence self-love becomes a threat to one's eternal life because it is not a true love.

It is love for fame for the image of the self in front of people, not for its eternity and purity. It is not a spiritual love and so, it is dangerous and causes harm. We can say that it is not love but a spiritual war.

The effort to magnify oneself through love of praise is a war in which many fall.

Whoever loves praise is not satisfied with being praised by people but proceeds to talk and praise themselves before others!

They are not unbiased in talking about themselves and do not tell the whole truth about themselves. They speak only of their own good qualities, victories, and glories, whilst at the same time, they conceals their defects. If someone were to reveal any of such defects, they try to justify and defend themselves.

It Is An Old War

It is the war which confronted our forefathers Adam and Eve when the devil tempted them saying, *"…you will be like God, knowing good and evil,…" (Gen.3:5).*

As man was tempted with self-exaltation, much earlier the devil himself fell from the same thoughts:

"For you have said in your heart, I will ascend into heaven, I will exalt my throne above the stars of God. I will ascend above

the heights of the clouds. I will be like the Most High." *(Isa.14:13,14).*

The repetition of the words *'ascend,' 'above,'* and *'height',* demonstrate an attempt to exalt oneself.

Exalting the self here amounts even to edifying it, *"I will be like the Most High".*

Is there a greater danger than such exaltation or such a drop? Herod the King was fought with this war and the angel of the Lord smote him, so he was eaten of worms and died (Acts 12:22,23).

One of the aspects of exalting the self is self-righteousness. This is mentioned in the Book of Job; *"So these three men ceased answering Job because he was righteous in his own eyes." (Job.32:*1). He was even rebuked by Elihu who said to Job, *"Do you say, My righteousness is more than God's..." (Job.35:*1).

Another example of self-exaltation in the Old Testament is the story of the Tower of Babylon. This story tells us that the people said, *"Come, let us build ourselves a city, and a tower whose top is in the heavens; let us make a name for ourselves. (Gen.11:4).*

But God punished the pride of these people. He confused their language and scattered them abroad upon the face of the earth.

This leads us to another point which is….

Self-Love Leads To Conflict With God

When a person trusts themselves only, they proceed to act independently, pursing their own wishes and this drives them away from God.

They trust their own judgment without consulting God. They say, *'As long as I understand what is best, why would I require knowledge from God or seek His help?'*.

Hence, a confident person finds it difficult to lead a life of submission.

A life of submission requires a humble heart which does not cling to one's own view. As such, it is completely opposed to the war of the 'self.'

Here, we remember the fault of Jonah the Prophet, who fled from the presence of God because he followed his own will that contradicted God's will. When God forgave Nineveh, Jonah was exceedingly displeased and angry, even to the point that he wanted to die. God then rebuked him saying, *"Is it right for you to be angry..." (Jon 4:1)."*

It truly is a sorrowful thing that a person becomes so angry because of God's will that they want to die. But it is the 'self!' Even a great prophet like Jonah was fought by the self so how much more are we subject to it.

There is another level to the war of the self which is the complete refusal of God.

Atheists made this terrible mistake due to their own lusts. They imagined that God's existence stood in the way of their free will. They imagined that God's love was against their desires and against their self-assurance. They envisioned His love as a deterrent from a life of pleasure, enjoyment, and a life of absolute freedom. They wanted to do whatever they desired, even though it would be against ideals, morals, principles and even against God's commandments.

Absolute freedom acquired by the self is one of the wars that aims at anarchism and ends in atheism. People involved in this or similar paths, ultimately reach a similar end - a matter which has been greatly regretted.

Theologians who gave themselves unlimited freedom concerning dogma are of this type. Any Biblical doctrines not accepted by them were refused or considered to be a myth. Sometimes they tried to interpret such doctrines to fit their trends. The story of Noah's ark was not accepted by their minds, so they considered it a mere myth.

With other types of people, the self undertook a new path whereby it contradicted God's commandments but in a much lighter way. An example are those people who break the commandment of the Lord's day because of the self and its engagements. Another example are those who break the commandment of the tithes because of the self and their expenditure. In these cases, the self conflicts with God with respect to conduct, not with respect to dogma.

+ Self-Love And The Confession Father.

A self-confident person looks at the confession father as a mere duty officer and confession as a formality. They do not seek the guidance of their confession father because they think they know everything and have a solution for every problem. They do not ask their confession father to lead them in their spiritual life because they know how to proceed and knows what is better! All that they want from the confession father is to agree to what they suggest, thereby completing their required obligation to confess. If the confession father does not agree with them, they argue and persist. They go on explaining and giving practical objections to the other solutions offered by the confession father to confirm their own opinion.

In short, we can say that obedience is difficult for a person who is subject to the war of the self, for they always behave according to their own will.

They think for themselves and whatever thought comes to them from others, they consider it as a mere suggestion which they are not obliged to take on board. Since this is their conduct with their confession father, they will undoubtedly apply the same principles in all their life.

Hence, we often see a self-confident person conflicting with their colleagues at work. They may also clash with their colleagues, feeling that they interfere with their work.

Self-Admiration

Self-admiration and egocentricity are due to some of the following: Superiority, talents, unusual abilities, or the feeling of power.

All these are characteristics that fight a person within and may express themselves externally. A self-admiring person will labour in this way to prove that they are endowed with talents and abilities.

Such wars become more severe if a person continually compares themselves to others.

Here, a person may feel superior to others in anything. This could be in intelligence, experience, power, beauty, or even talent such as drawing, music, poetry, handwork or languages etc.

Even in the service of God, the self may feel distinguished if a person believes that they have more abilities in ministry than others.

For example, a person may be able to learn hymns, has a sweeter voice, surpasses others in the study of the Holy Bible or in being acquainted with the sayings of the fathers. They may also be more effective in their service, in preaching, in management or in planning.

Self-admiration also comes from positions, prestige, wealth, or fame.

Such matters may be causes for self-admiration but the humble escape them. They do this by serving others genuinely and not as a means for showing off, boasting, or exalting themselves.

There is no doubt that talents also have their danger.

Talents may exalt the heart internally and perhaps externally. It may also lead to the war of vain glory. Here, one may inquire how could a person endowed by God with the gift of doing miracles endure this, especially if this gift was raising the dead or opening the eyes of the blind? So, one of the fathers said;

'If you are endowed by God with some gift, pray to Him to give it with humility which would preserve it or ask Him to take it away.'

Hence, we are amazed at those who ask God for the gift of talking in various tongues or other gifts, instead of praying for purity of heart and the fruits of the Spirit. Such people are not thinking of preaching in the wilderness of Africa, in China or in Japan but they only ask for the gift for itself. Yet brother, what benefit do these gifts avail you? They may be a war against you. Why would your heart be distressed without them? Listen to the Lord commanding us to seek first God's kingdom and Righteousness.

However, if by God's divine dispensation we are given such surpassing gifts, let us pray to be given humility with them, so that the self vanishes.

As for you, my beloved brother, if you are fought with this war, ask yourself, *'Am I able to endure such a gift or would it lead to pride and make me lose my eternity?'*

Results Of Self-Worship

A Self-confident person is subject to obstinacy and stubbornness.

Their views are above all others and they do not accept any opposition. Whoever opposes them becomes their enemy; they may hate them or try to destroy them. At the very least, they neglect opposing opinions. This is over-confidence in one's intelligence or knowledge and it is extremely hard to deal with such a person.

Such people continually interrupt a person talking with them. They insist on their own views though others give strong evidence for them to consider. As a result, people avoid such personalities and avoid any discussion with them, seeing there is no use.

A self-confident person may be domineering when they attain a leading position. This domineering quality comes not only from stubbornness but also from insisting on carrying out one's opinion, maybe even by force.

This may even happen in the field of ministry, where some minister disregards the personality of other ministers and cancel any discussion with them! *'Their attitude is, 'It's my way and not yours or anyone else's!'*

Here, self-worship would surely lead to conceit, pride, and arrogance.

A person in such cases criticizes the life of meekness, humility and calmness and moves from domination to edification.

Another aspect of self-love is false self-satisfaction.

False Self-Satisfaction

This means satisfying oneself through pleasure, not through pride.

Both matters can be found in the words of St. John, "*...the lust of the flesh, the lust of the eyes, and the pride of life.' '(John 2:16).* Thus, adultery is a war of the self and lust for food is another war which fights the flesh.

Wars of the self may attack the body or the soul. Satisfaction of the body may take the form of having the inability to fast due to the greed of delicious foods, wine or for narcotics which may lead to addiction.

It would take long to talk about lusts of the flesh and now is not the time for it.

The Self And Giving

Self-love stands as an insurmountable barrier against love of others, against the life of sacrifice and against giving. An example of this is the foolish rich man who neglected Lazarus the poor (Luke 16). Another example is the greedy and the materialistic and those who neglect to pay the firstlings, tithes, and vow offerings.

However, a self-lover may give but within certain limits which do not affect them or their desires. They may give of their abundance but can never give out of their need, like the holy widow whom the Lord of glory praised (Luke 21:4). Whatever they give is outside themselves but they can never give themselves.

A self-lover will not sacrifice themselves for the sake of others. They will not give themselves to redeem others. When such a person finds any danger in defending others they withdraw because their self is more important to them! Truly, self-love leads to the rejection of scarifies, redemption or a brave defense of others.

The self may also impede ministry under the pretext of lack of time. A self-lover gives ministry the remainder of their time. They will only serve if it is convenient not out of sacrifice. They may give excuses to leave their ministry and not to meet its obligations; they neglect the times of service and prefer any other engagements, disregarding the impact on the ministry.

If a person cannot sacrifice for service what would they do in front of martyrdom? A self-lover cannot give themselves up to be martyred because their self is dear to them. So a martyr has to first get rid of self-love and vain concern for their well-being. A martyr gives themselves up for the sake of God.

There is a lesser rank of martyrdom which is giving oneself to God through consecration.

Consecration is a high rank of ministry in which a consecrated person gives all his time to God. They can only do this if the self vanishes. It is not consecration when the self is magnified but true consecration is when the self is sacrificed. A person who has self-denial gives the best of what they has.

Such a person does not seek glory or honour for themselves but gives out of concern for those they are serving as the Apostle says, *"Love... does not seek its own" (Cor. 13).*

A self-lover will prioritise the best for themselves.

The worst case of self-love is when a person gives and later regrets that they gave and then retrieves it.

Now, we move to another point.

Faults Of The Self In Its Dealings With Others

Sometimes a self-loving person finds it necessary to struggle against others to assert themselves. The first step towards this is competition. If competition is for public benefit such that all compete in serving the society, it is good. This is just as the Holy Bible says, *"But it is good to be zealous in a good thing always..." (Gal 4:18).*

But if competition is an attempt by one party to conquer the other by any means necessary, even by destroying it, then the self here is accompanied by lack of love for others.

It is good that everyone competes to become better but the danger of self-love appears when one hates others who surpass them. Selfishness here leads to envy, jealousy and hatred.

A jealous person wants to have everything, leaving everyone else with nothing. They want to be exalted and to dominate alone. To alone be superior and praised, having the spotlight focused on them. Otherwise, the self would wage a war against whoever rivals it or whoever takes the same course.

There are types of people who want to be exalted while others want exaltation for themselves only. Here, the danger lies in the fact that such a type of self resists others despite them being blameless and loving, committing no fault against them or against others.

It is a cross the outstanding persons bear as a result of those who envy them. This is what David the Prophet suffered from King Saul and what Joseph the Righteous suffered from his brothers. For the same reason, Herod rose against the Lord Jesus Christ at His birth. Also the Pharisees out of envy said among themselves, *"'You see that you are accomplishing nothing. Look, the world has gone after him!" (John 12:19).*

How sad to read these words in Genesis, *"Now the land was not able to support them that they might dwell together." (Gen.13:6).*

If the self wants to dominate, it is ready to destroy whoever competes with it, as in the case of Ahab the King who killed Naboth the Jezreelite. (1 Kings 21:1-16)

The same can be said concerning respect and praise.

We have seen one of the problems of the self-loving person i.e. their love to be praised by people and to have their concern and respect. Here we see a more dangerous type; a person who wants themselves alone to be respected, cared for and praised. The matter would be even worse if such feeling leads them to enmity with anyone because of this. Hence conflicts exist among persons of the same profession or who work in the same field or who compete for supremacy.

Mary sat at the feet of the Lord Jesus Christ listening to Him and did nothing against Martha. Yet, she did not escape her criticism. It is the self that made Martha criticize her sister Mary saying within herself, *'Why would I work alone? Won't she come and work with me.'* Or *'Why would she enjoy the gathering with Jesus while I am deprived of it?'* (Luke 10:40).

As Martha criticized Mary due to envy, so the elder son criticized his younger brother, the prodigal son (Luke15).

Another point concerning self-love is that a self-lover never blames themselves but…**They throws the responsibility of his faults on others.**

If such a person fails in an exam, they say that either the examiner set a difficult exam or that they were marked unfairly. They may even say that perhaps God did not help them in spite of the prayers they offered.

Such a person always feels that they are persecuted. If a self-loving person does not gain what they want they resent, grumble and complain.

They accuse their parents, accuse society and accuses the times they live in. They accuse the treatment of others and give many causes for their not attaining their goals. They criticise anyone who attains a high position and criticises the means used, showing themselves beyond such means.

Their self alone is excused and that does no wrong!!!

Thus they cannot correct any of their faults because their self is blameless in their own eyes. As their troubles continue, without being corrected, their complaints continue without end.

If they are in authority, they complain of the faults of their subordinates. If they are a subordinate, they complain of those in authority and of their colleagues. If they find nothing wrong with those, they complain of the rules, the laws and the regulations! In short, they defend themselves when they do anything wrong and covers their fault with lies or different excuses.

A self-loving person is very sensitive about their dignity. They treat people with scales different from those which they treat themselves. They examine carefully any word addressed to them but are not mindful of what they say to others. They want to be treated in a way that is different from the way they treat others. They are sensitive about their dignity but not about the dignity of others.

On the following pages I shall talk to you about self-denial and self-condemnation; how and when one can possess such attributes.

Self-Denial

The Great Model

Since the first man was conquered in the war of the self, coveting to be like God (Gen. 3:5), the Lord Jesus Christ, who blessed our nature in Himself, corrected this fault. How did that take place? The Apostle tells us; *"But made Himself of no reputation, taking the form of a servant, and coming in the likeness of men."* *(Phil.2:7).*

He lived on earth in poverty, had *"...nowhere to lay His head."* (Luke9:58). He held no official position and renounced His

60

dignity, *"He was oppressed and He was afflicted, yet He opened not His mouth.. and He was numbered with the transgressors."* *(Isa.53:7,12).*

He did not defend Himself.

He denied Himself for our sakes. He humbled Himself to raise us up. He stood as a transgressor so that we may be made righteous. He had no regard for Himself but for us.

Although John the Baptist baptized the Lord a baptism of repentance, the Lord Jesus Christ had no need to repent or to be baptized accordingly, yet He came to be baptized for our sakes. In self-denial He said to John, His servant, *"Permit it to be so now,..."*. *(Matt.3:15).*

The Lord's humbling Himself is a long subject which has no place here. You can read about it in my book "Contemplations on the Nativity" (Pages7-28).

Let's here deal with other aspects of self-denial.

+ Self-Sacrifice.

Self-sacrifice may be for God's sake, for the church or for any person whether a relative or a stranger. See how beautiful the words of St. Paul the Apostle are in this concern;

"... nor do I count my life dear to myself,.." *(Acts.20:24)* and the Apostle laboured tirelessly in ministry, *"In journeys often in perils of waters, in perils of robbers, in perils of my own countrymen, in perils of Gentiles, in perils in the city, in perils in*

the wilderness, in perils in the sea, in perils among false brethren; in weariness and toil, in sleeplessness often, in hunger and thirst, in fasting often, in cold and .. nakedness" (II Cor.11:26,27), "...in tribulations in needs, in distresses; in stripes, in imprisonments..." (2Cor.6:4,5).

Thus, the Apostle is a model for ministry that seeks not rest but gives itself and toils in preaching and teaching and in searching for the lost.

He was like the candle which melts to give light to people, and like the incense which burns to give a sweet smell to others.

We put this example before a person who insists on being consecrated in a large country, or a rich church or in a church near to his house!

For the sake of preaching, the Apostles wandered as strangers in far countries. Some of them preached the word among cannibals; their main concern being to spread God's word.

What of you, if you are called to serve, do not think of yourself or of your comfort or your needs whether financial or material, for God takes care of all this. Give all your concern for the souls in need for God. Search for the needy districts and the places that do not have anyone to serve them whatever effort you have to exert for this purpose.

In the field of ministry remember the words of the Lord, *"He who finds his life will lose it, and he who loses his life for My sake will find it." (Matt.10:39).*

What do these beautiful words mean? What is the spiritual depth behind them? What examples explain them?

Who Loses Themselves

Perhaps some thought that Moses the Prophet had destroyed himself when he refused the monarchy and the King's palace because of his holy Zeal!! *"Choosing rather to suffer affliction with the people of God... esteeming the reproach of Christ greater riches than the treasures in Egypt." (Heb.11:25,26).*

However, the soul of Moses was not lost; he found it in the comfort of others, in converting them to the faith and in God's work through him. He became the pioneer of faith in his days. He was also the first person whom God entrusted with His written law.

He was on the Mount of Transfiguration with the Lord Jesus Christ and Elijah. As for the monarchy which he had lost, it was a mere trifle compared to the glories which he obtained.

However, Moses was not thinking of those glories when he left Pharaoh's Palace. He only wanted to sacrifice himself for the sake of the people choosing rather to suffer affliction with them than to enjoy palaces!!

The same happened with our father Abraham who was called by God. In fact, he was called to leave his kindred and his father's house and become a stranger in a land which he did not know (Gen. 12).

Afterwards God gave him an even harder test - to offer his only son as a sacrifice.

Abraham's obedience to sacrifice became a shining example throughout the ages and God rewarded him with descendants as numerous as the stars of heaven and as the sand which is on the seashore. We are all sons of Abraham (Rom.4:11,16).

Was Abraham thinking of himself when he lifted up his hand with the knife to slay his son? No, He was not thinking at all of himself but God's commandment was the only thing before his eyes. This was also his feeling when he left his country not knowing where he was going (Heb.11:8). But God provides a reward for him who had sacrificed and for whoever may sacrifice.

Sacrifice yourself then and be sure that your self will be very dear and valuable in the sight of God and He will not let it perish. He will restore to you a hundred-fold and you will find yourself in Him.

Now, we come to another point concerning self-denial.

Asceticism And Forsaking Pleasures

A person whose only concern is themselves and their lusts, acts as Solomon the Wise described; *"I built myself houses and planted myself vineyards. I made myself gardens and orchards... Whatever my eyes desired I did not keep from them... "* (Eccl. 2:4-10).

Here are the worldly and fleshly pleasures of the self to which the words of the Lord apply, *"He who finds his life will lose it..."* *(Matt.10:39).*

As opposed to this is forsaking food, clothing and everything. Those who lead a life of pleasure receive their good things on earth, as it was said to the rich man in the story of Lazarus the Poor (Luke 16:25). On the other hand those who forsake pleasures obtain their reward with God in heaven.

We find in the stories of the father monks, the anchorites and the solitary, wonderful examples of the ascetic life where self is forsaken with all its lusts.

There are models of ascetics who lived in kings' palaces, such as Daniel the Prophet who, *"Purposed that he would not defile himself with the portion of the king's delicacies, nor with the wine which he drank." (Dan.1:8).* Daniel himself said of his fast, *"I ate no pleasant food, no meat or wine came into my mouth, nor did I anoint myself at all, till three whole weeks were fulfilled." (Dan. 10:3).*

Where is the self here, in the case of such a person as Daniel, who lived in a king's palace refusing all delicacies and was satisfied with vegetables alone! Though Daniel was a ruler, he ate no pleasant food.

Fasting attempts to attain control of the self and chastity.

+ Controlling The Self

Fasting and chastity are aspects of controlling the self with respect to the desires and lusts of the body. There is also another aspect with respect to the soul.

Happy is the person who controls themselves and prevents the self from deviating towards worldly pleasures. The self may tend to ostentation, showing off and arrogance and in all this it must resist. You have to convince yourself that it is better for you to be pleased with God and have rewards in the coming life.

Those who want to have pleasure here are faced with the words of the Lord, *"Truly, I say to you, they have their reward..."* *(Matt.6:5)*.

Do not try then to obtain all your rights on earth. It is better for you to have them there, where God will wipe away every tear from your eyes.

If your self or your body are inclined to the pleasures of this present world, prevent them strongly. This is not cruelty towards your self or your body but it is to ensure eternal life for them.

Those who spoil themselves here cause their own destruction and he who slackens in restraining the self, gives it power over him and makes it rebel against his spirit.

Be sure that self-vanquishing gives a spiritual pleasure incomparable to all fleshly enjoyment.

I think I have talked to you about self-vanquishing before, in a previous lecture about, *'attaining by force'*.

It is very strange when someone strives very hard to show off, even in ministry, when we should be striving to vanquish the self

Self In The Field Of Ministry

When the devil finds someone on their guard, vanquishing themselves with respect to all fleshly pleasures, they attempt another war. They provide the person with an opportunity to show off in the field of ministry.

It is easy for a person serving in the church to have an occasion to glorifying the self, show off and gain gratification.

How easy it is for a person giving a sermon to use it to boast about their knowledge and reveal their talents and understanding, even though their words have little effect on the salvation of those listening and may also be far from the subject of the sermon! Here the devil stands laughing because he has caused the servant to sin and the hearers of the sermon to gain no benefit!

How easy it is for a minister to attach the congregation they serve to themselves, not to God. They may form factions between the congregation to support them when they get into trouble. Here the self is obviously apparent. A spiritual person is not like this at all.

Spiritual persons take the sermon as a faithful attempt to go into the depths of the soul in order to purify it and attach it to God. They urge people by any means or style to leave their sins, to love God and love doing good.

What concerns such spiritual persons is the spiritual objective.

There is a great difference between a sermon which leaves the listeners saying, *'what a learned preacher that person was!'* and sermon which leaves them saying *'We want to repent'.!*

The self of the preacher, the instructor or the evangelist is not the aim but salvation of souls is the true aim. A successful preacher is one who gains souls for the Lord not he who gains personal praise from his listeners. How beautiful are the words of the Psalmist in this respect; *"Not unto us, 0 Lord, not unto us, But to Your name give glory." (Ps.115:1).*

The purpose of a sermon is to reveal to the listener their self and their spiritual wars; to teach them how to condemn themselves and overcome themselves. A sermon is not meant to give a person knowledge for which he will not be asked about at the final judgment!

If every preacher removes their self while delivering a sermon and concentrates on the salvation of others, many would gain the Kingdom of heaven.

In the field of ministry, we have the example of St. John the Baptist whose words about the Lord were truly great;

"He must increase, but I must decrease." (John 3:30).

St John used to turn all the love of people to the Lord Jesus Christ and hide himself because he did not come to witness for himself but, *"To bear witness of the light that all through him might believe..." (John 1:7).*

St. John came to prepare people to receive the Lord Jesus Christ and *"...to make ready a people prepared for the Lord." (Luke 1:17).* He succeeded in the message of hiding himself. Here we state an important fact:

There are two matters through which ministry succeeds.

1- God must be the aim.

2- God must be the way and the self must not be an aim or a means.

We say this because many people depend mainly upon themselves in the ministry. They depend upon their intelligence, their knowledge, their personal influence, their fame and dignity, all of which make their behaviour and words acceptable...! But where is God?

As God is not present in ministry, it fails and the self appears. Also usually prayers decrease and so the ministry becomes weak because God does not bless it.

The ministry of spiritual persons has a certain impression as you feel it is God who works and blesses every step.

Hence also there is peace, love and cooperation in the field of ministry.

Not only does everyone hide their self so that God may appear but also everyone hides to promote others above themselves. This is true humility and service.

On the other hand, if there exists Paul and Apollos in ministry, the self exists and with it divisions appear. (ICor.3:3,4).

So, when the Lord's disciples desired to know who was the first among them, the Lord taught them the error of this and said;

Yet it shall not be so among you, but whoever desires to become great among you, let him be your servant... Just as the Son of Man did not come to be served, but to serve, and to give His life a ransom for many." (Matt.20:26-28).

Listen also to the beautiful words of a spiritual elder;

'Wherever you settle, be the youngest of your brothers and a servant to them'.

Love of supremacy is a severe war which may ruin ministry. Competition and showing off are also due to the self and may lead to the same.

The Lord Jesus Christ gave as a remedy for all this, the principle of, "...*sitting down in the lowest place..." (Luke 14:10).*

+ The Lowest Place

We mean here to take the lowest rank or position.

Do not esteem yourself as the most important of all among your brothers. Do not consider your opinion, your decision or your position as the most important. Do not think that you are more capable than all others, that you must be obeyed and respected and if not, you get angry and furious!!

Do not give yourself dignity and impose it upon others but let them honour you for the meekness and humility they see in you.

Do not force people to respect you, for respect must come from the heart, not by force but by personal esteem. You may force someone to obey you but cannot force them to respect you.

Force here is a kind of domination. In your dealings with others, be a breeze not a storm! Many like to be a storm because power is its quality but the breeze symbolises meekness and gentleness. Anyone who denies themself must be meek and gentle.

In dealing with others do not favour yourself.

The Apostle says, *"...in honor giving preference to one another..." (Rom.12:10)*.

This must be from the depth of your heart, in deep humility and without flattery...

Another lesson concerning dealing with others is offered us by the Lord in the Sermon on the Mount and that is:

The Second Mile

The Lord says, *"If anyone wants to sue you and take away your tunic, let him have your cloak also. And whoever compels you to go one mile; go with him two." (Matt. 5;40,41)*.

In the same spirit the Lord tells us about giving the other cheek; *"But whoever slaps you on your right cheek turn the other to him also..." (Matt. 5.:39)*. By all this the Lord seems to say,

'Be oppressed rather than oppressor. Be crucified not a crucifier. Do not avenge yourself.'

The self wants to have its rights, here, on earth and as soon as possible.

But the Lord teaches us, saying, *"Resist not evil..." (Matt.5:39).*

Do not fight or insist to have your rights or to avenge, and remember the words of the Holy Bible, *"Vengeance is Mine, I will repay, says the Lord,..." (Rom.12:19).* And though vengeance is the Lord's, do not demand it from Him, as the Holy Bible tells us, *"Love... does not seek its own..." (1Cor.3:5).*

Why does it not seek its own? That is because it is void of the self.

As you are required not to glorify yourself, you are also required to condemn yourself.

The biggest problem in all one's dealings is to always think that you are right!

Self-condemnation

Such a person does not apologize when they do anything wrong because they always think themselves right. When they clash with their brother, they don't take the initiative to reconcile with them. They expect the initiative to come from the other party! Why? It is their self.

Even with God, they may not confess their faults because their self convinces them that they did no wrong.

Self-condemnation comes from humility and humility leads to self-denial. A person who is not humble does not condemn or blame themselves; they always condemn and blame others!!

If you ask such a person why they blame others, they reproach you for saying so.

A person who does not seek always to glorify and magnify themselves through worldly methods and whose objective is to purify themselves of any faults or defects always blames themselves, examines their faults and condemns themselves for spiritual benefit.

Once Pope Theophilus (of the fourth Century) visited the area of the 'Cells' in Mount Nitria and asked a blessed elder, *""What thing of excellence have you found on this road?"* (monastic path) *And the old man said, "I make accusations against myself, and I blame myself at all times.""* (The Paradise of the Holy Fathers Vol. 2 pp. 108-109)

That is the spiritual way by which one attempts to refine oneself; to blame oneself and not make excuses of their surrounding circumstances or God!

Whoever condemns themselves here, shall be saved from condemnation in the age to come. Why? Because a person who condemns themselves will easily repent and through repentance their sins shall be forgiven by the Lord. On the other hand, a person who does not condemn themselves, remains in sin and is under condemnation.

See the true words of St. Anthony;

'If we condemn ourselves, the Judge will be pleased with us. If we remember our sins, God will forget them; but if we forget our sins, God will remember them for us.'

Self-condemnation helps us to reconcile with people. If you apologise to someone saying, 'You are right. I was wrong concerning this matter!' This would stop their anger and make them reconcile with you. But if you insist on justifying yourself, you will cause an argument and further conflict. How beautiful are the words of St. Macarius the Great in this respect;

'Brother, condemn yourself before others condemn you!'

CHAPTER 3

EMPTINESS

Many spiritual wars fight a person in their spiritual journey; some of which come from within and others from without. Some wars are from devils and some from our surroundings. We shall deal here with emptiness as one of these wars.

Emptiness is of various types.

Spare Time

A person who has a lot of spare time may fall into various spiritual faults if they use their time in a wrong way.

When God created our father Adam, He did not leave him with nothing to do but gave him work. The Holy Bible says; *"Then the Lord God took the man and put him in the garden of Eden to tend and keep it." (Gen. 2:15).* Adam and Eve did not need to earn their living because there was abundance in paradise. They were given work to avoid being idle. I think sin fought them while they were unemployed because if they had been busy at the time the devil tempted them, they might not have fallen.

Even monks have to work as part of their lives provided that it does not hinder their spiritual practices.

Manual work is mentioned in the *Paradise of the Holy Fathers* as essential for monks. It is still practiced by them until now. The reason is that when a monk starts their monastic life, they don't have the ability to spend all their time in prayers. They are given some work by the monastery lest idleness should destroy their salvation. Work also allows a monk to take part in the service of the monastery and to show love for their brethren. It allows them also to discover their own faults through dealing with others.

Having too much spare time makes a person feel bored and makes them lazy, so they seek amusement to comfort them. Very often when looking for amusement, one may choose something wrong or inappropriate.

A person may hold idle conversations with others which would waste both their time and may cause people to tire of them. They may also go to places of entertainment, coffee houses or clubs where they find many opportunities for wrongdoing. Some may just wonder the streets for pleasure without an aim calling it, 'taking a walk'.

A person may also spend a lot of time with others, wasting their time as well.

Wasting time in such a way, without any occupation, is wasting part of one's life!! Our lives should be made use of for our own benefit and the benefit of others.

No doubt, a person who wastes their time is not aware of the value of their life and probably have no meaningful aims to achieve. As opposed to this is the person who puts before them a meaningful aim and makes use of all their time in order to achieve it. They may even need more time but don't find it.

So, you have to fill your spare time (and that of your children if you have them) with something useful.

Perhaps you sometimes get annoyed of the noise made by children and begin blaming, rebuking, shouting and giving them moral lessons. You pour on them your orders and prohibitions, your punishments and threats. The probable cause for the children's misbehavior is that they have nothing productive to occupy their time. If you are able to fill their time productively both you and they will be relieved. Therefore, think how best to occupy your children's' spare time.

Now, let me ask, 'How do you spend your spare time? In the right way? In a useful way?'

Do you make use of such time for your spiritual or mental growth or for the service of others or in exercise or hobbies which are not harmful, or in showing love to people and visiting them? Or is your spare time wasted perhaps in listening to the radio or watching T.V or the internet, which may not only take your spare time but may also consume all e of your time, even the part necessary for carrying out your responsibilities? Here I may ask, 'Do you fall in spiritual emptiness while treating the problem of your spare time?'

Emptiness Of Mind

Sometimes your being idle in your spare time will lead to emptiness of your mind. Here the devil comes to occupy the mind and distract it or tempt it, as the saying tells us, *'The mind of the lazy is a laboratory for the devil.'*. So, solitude or seclusion without spiritual work is very dangerous. For if there is no spiritual thought to control the mind, it will go astray and indulge a sinful thought.

Solitude in its spiritual meaning is to be alone with God; So it is not Emptiness.

Another type of emptiness of mind is its lack of knowledge; that is useful knowledge.

A person who is not assiduous in cultivating his mind with useful spiritual, ecclesiastical and general knowledge, will be ignorant and find nothing deep or useful to say to others.

The education of woman brought her out of this emptiness of mind that she was subject to in the dark ages. Education of a countries people also removed them from emptiness of mind.

Service of the word is very necessary to bring people out of emptiness of mind, unless what is told them is not useful. This is what happens to ministers who do not diligently prepare their sermons. Like them are those who present repeated familiar knowledge which has no depth, no novelty and no influence. Like them also are those who speak with no spirit in them, having only knowledge and information that does not enter into the heart and leaves the spirit empty. This leads us to another point:

Spiritual Emptiness

God created the soul in His image after His likeness, so nothing can satisfy the soul except God alone.

A soul that lives away from God's love feels emptiness. Regardless of whatever emotions are offered to it, it is not satisfied.

There may be some whose time is fully occupied with many engagements and serious responsibilities to carry out. They may have vast knowledge and have undertaken deep studies, yet they live in spiritual emptiness. Nothing they do can satisfy their soul.

Such people may spend their lives struggling for various

objectives of which they achieve some only.

But there remains in their hearts a desire not yet realized which always gives them the feeling of spiritual emptiness. Such a desire will never be satisfied except through deep attachment to God and firm love for Him.

If the souls of those people were released from their bodies and their materialistic life, they will certainly feel how empty they were. All worldly matters that they experienced did not fill part of this emptiness. So, from now, while we are still in this world, let us respond to the words of the Apostle;

"Be filled with the Spirit." (Eph.5:18).

It avails you nothing to fill your life with many things and not fill your heart with God.

How easy it is for a person to turn into a machine rotating all the time without spiritual purpose. God looks down upon such a person and finds them empty in spite of the abundant work they perform. Hence he hears from God the same words addressed to the elder of the church of the Laodiceans, *"...Because you say' I am rich, have become wealthy, and have need of nothing and do not know that you are wretched, miserable, poor, blind and naked.".*

Therefore, be filled with the love and knowledge of God because without it your souls will feel empty.

It is not sufficient for you to taste how good the Lord is but you must be filled with Him. If you are filled with God, you will be able to overflow to others. The love which is in you will fill their hearts with love and the peace within you will fill their lives with peace. The spirit they have would lead them to live in spirit.

How beautiful it would be when your soul ascends to God that it would be full of love, happiness, peace and faith besides all the other fruits of the Spirit (Gal.5:22).

Be filled with spiritual nourishment so that your souls may be filled with the fruits of the Spirit. This is what is done for a tree! We provide it with the necessary water and manure so that it may give you the flowers and fruit you desire.

Now, do you feel emptiness of spirit? Be filled then with all the means of grace. Provide your soul with deep spiritual material and in the foremost the word of God. Provide for yourself the contemplations, prayers, hymns, Psalms and spiritual songs it needs (Eph. 5:19).

Do not leave your soul empty or lacking any of the work of grace.

Strength of spirit makes the personality strong while lack of spirit leads to emptiness of personality.

This leads to the next topic, of having a weak personality.

Weak Personality

How hard it is for a person to feel that they have a weak personality, of no value in their society, bearing no fruit and having no influence.

A person may have this feeling within themselves and as a result may be mean-spirited seeing that they have no depth, no thought, no knowledge, no personality and no power!

Instead of strengthening their personality or giving it depth, they may add to it another weakness but in vain. For example, they may live in an imaginary world trying to please themselves with daydreams. However, these dreams are of no use to them because when they stop day-dreaming they find the painful reality of their weakness of personality unchanged

Another person may try to use excessive talk or useless conversation in the hope that it would create for them a personality. People may get bored with their conversation seeing it as idle and wasting of time.

A person may also use self-praise to cover their weak personality. They boast of their 'great' works or attributes when they aren't so great. They may also rebuke others criticism so that they look more knowledgeable. They may resist those who work because they are jealous that they have meaningful work while they are doing nothing.

They may sit arrogantly concealing their weak personality with wealth and elegance acting elite in their appearance and by the way they talk!

Another similar example is the woman who conceals her weak personality by making a great effort towards her looks and attire, through makeup, jewelry and fashionable clothes. The Psalms address a woman's beauty by saying;

"The king's daughter is all glorious within..." (Ps. 45:13).

I wish that society would treat those people suffering from a weak personality by finding them something to occupy their minds and make use of their abilities. I wish that everybody would discover his own abilities and try to make good use of them. Whoever feels that they have a weak personality needs to work to better it instead of trying to conceal it.

Every person has to ask themselves daily what useful thing they have done that day. They should try to do something good, not only to satisfy themselves but also out of love for good and for people. By doing this they will feel satisfied without seeking it.

I wish that there would be a meaningful aim for everybody who strives hard to achieve one. As long as this aim is spiritual and useful, working for it will save the person from the feeling of emptiness.

Hence, we say that ambition is a remedy for the feeling of emptiness, provided that it is proper and free from vanity and selfishness.

Emotional Emptiness

It is of two kinds:

The first kind is the person who feels within themselves a great heart but finds no one to fill it.

They want to give their love to someone but they don't know where. So they feel empty with respect to giving. This type is easily cured.

If such a person can give their love in the field of ministry, no doubt they will feel happy. The service of children satisfies the heart, the same as the service of the orphans, the needy, the poor, the handicapped, the sick and whoever is in need. They can also give by solving people's problems.

The second kind are those who feel in need of love but find no one to love them.

An example of this type is a daughter who lives in a house void of love. The father is very firm and harsh, always rebuking and punishing. The mother also is cruel and the daughter finds no kindness at all from her. Many are the girls who deviate because they find no love or kindness from the parents or the family! While in this psychological condition, that girl may find someone who offers her the wrong kind of love or another kind of love. She accepts it and even seeks' it because she needs a heart.... any heart.

Here, we advise parents to give love to their sons and daughters to protect them from this. At the same time, we urge sons and daughters to seek love in a proper chaste way.

Surely, they will find this in the love of God and His Kingdom, in pure innocent friendships and also in the field of ministry and giving.

Those who give to others holy love and kindness, will receive the same and more than what they have given.

The point is to fill the heart with emotions whether taking or giving. Giving is at the same time taking.

David the Prophet found in the friendship of Jonathan love

surpassing the love of women (II Sam. 1:26). John the Beloved also found in the love of the Lord the greatest love in the world.

Those who live in monasticism and virginity found in the love of God something which made them forget all the universe and all that is in it.

How beautiful are the words of the spiritual father;

'God's love estranged me from human beings and human matters.'

CHAPTER 4

FORGETFULNESS

What Things Do You Forget?

One of the saints said, *"Every sin is preceded either by lust, ignorance or forgetfulness"*.

We shall discuss forgetfulness as a spiritual war which causes us to sin.

When we sin, we forget God, we forget the commandments and forget our spiritual life as a whole. We forget death and eternity and forget the spirits of the angels and the saints who see us in the very act!! If we remember all these things, we will not sin or at least will delay in committing sin, get ashamed or afraid or keep away from sin.

In fact, at the time of sin, none of these things come to our minds.

We are completely drugged by the devil in order to forget so that we can fulfill our lust.

A person forgets or feigns forgetfulness and does not like anyone to remind them of God, of the commandment, or of eternity. At the time of fast or feasts they forget that those are holy days. They forget the holy places and forget that they are the temple of God and God's spirit dwells in them. They forget the blood of the Lord Jesus Christ that was shed for them and forgets their promises and vows to God.

What is preaching but that a preacher reminds people of all this so that through remembrance they may keep away from sin out of fear, shame or bashfulness or keep themselves from falling.

God Reminds Us

As God knows the harms of forgetfulness and wants to save us, He gave us many things by which we may come to ourselves and be aware. But what are those things by which God remedies our forgetfulness?

God put a conscience within us to remind us of the way of righteousness.

A conscience is called *'the natural law'* by which God wrote down His law within our hearts. For example, Joseph the Righteous had no written law before him when he said, *"How then can I do this great wickedness, and sin against God? (Gen.39:9)*. But he did have the unwritten law within him i.e. the natural law which reminded him that this was a sin.

When people began to forget the natural law, God gave them, through Moses the Prophet, the first written law. God ordered us to put that law before us all the time so that we may not forget.

He said, *"And these words which I command you today shall be in your heart; you shall teach them diligently to your children and shall talk of them when you sit in your house, when you walk by the way, when you lie down, and when you rise up. You shall bind them as a sign on your hand, and they shall be as frontlets between your eyes. You shall write them on the doorposts of your house and on your gates." (Deut.6:6-9).*

All this is required in order that we may not forget the commandment. God ordered us also to meditate on His commandment day and night.

David the Prophet says of this, *"unless Your law had been my delight, I would then have perished in my affliction."* *(Ps.119:92).*

He says also of the righteous man in Psalm 1, *"But his delight is in the law of the Lord, and in His law he meditates day and night. He shall be like a tree planted by the rivers of water..." (Ps 1:2,3).*

Listen to the Lord saying to Joshua the Son of Nun, *"This Book of the Law shall not depart from your mouth, but you may observe to do according to all that is written in it." (Josh.1:8).*

When God found that the Five Books of the Law became too much for the people, He helped them to remember them by summing them up in one Book, namely Deuteronomy. A copy of Deuteronomy was usually given to every king so that he might read it continuously and not sin out of forgetfulness.

The commandments were also distributed in the Temple and Synagogues to be read by the people throughout the whole year lest they should forget them. Until today, we hear the commandments in the churches, in every liturgy and in every ritual prayer so that we may not forget.

In every Liturgy we listen to readings from the Holy Bible, the Epistles and the Psalms. In Lent and Paschal week, parts of the Old Testament are recited. On the Holy Saturday the Book of Revelation is read with hymns and prayers of the prophets. All this is also arranged by the church so that we may not forget.

In order that people may not forget, God sent them the prophets and Apostles. He even sent the Holy Spirit in order to, *"...bring to your remembrance all things that I said to you..." (Jn.14:26).*

For the same purpose, God sent pastors, preachers, teachers and all priestly ranks so that they may remind people of the word of God lest they should forget it. God called those 'ministers of the word' and St. Paul the Apostle says regarding this, *"...as though God were pleading through us..." (2Cor.5:20)*.

How beautiful also are the words of St. Evagrius;

"When any thought fights you, put before you one of the commandments and the thought will grow weak and you will overcome it."

In this way, the commandment will give you power, you will gain knowledge and enlightenment by which you can recognise the thought which attacks you and dismiss it. Listen to what St. Paul the Apostle says to comfort us;

"For the word of God is living and powerful, and sharper than any two-edged sword." (Heb.4:12).

In order not to forget, God gave us in the church the rites of special feasts and celebrations.

For example, in order for us not to forget His being crucified and to keep in mind the holy feelings arising from the events of His crucifixion, the church arranged for us the Passion Week as a yearly celebration, the fasts on Wednesdays and Fridays, as a weekly remembrance and the Sixth Hour Prayer as a daily remembrance.

The Church does not want us to forget the Holy Blood shed for us so that this might make us ashamed of sin.

So, a person who does not fast may forget and a person who fasts without understanding or depth may also forget. A person who does not pray the hourly prayers may forget as well.

How easy it is for those who do not practice the spiritual means to fall.

The Church Reminds Us

All celebrations of seasons and feasts held by the church remind us of useful facts of faith and arouse within us spiritual feelings which may prevent us from sinning.

The same can be said of fasting, of church rituals, church prayers and the use of candles, icons and incense in church.

So, days of fasting are spiritual days that keep many wars away from us, or at least remind us that the spirit must overcome the fleshly desires, not only for food but all other evil desires

Icons remind us of the lives of the saints so that we can learn from them and take their lives as an example for our own lives. Their lives are as a sweet-smelling aroma for our spiritual journey.

Candles remind us that we are the light of the world (Matt.5:14) and to sacrifice ourselves to give light to others.

Candles also remind us of the angels and how the church resembles heaven and we, like stars, give light in heaven. Candles remind us of the word of God which shines and gives light to the eyes (Ps. 19) as David the prophet says, *"Your word is a lamp to my feet and a light to my path." (Ps.119:105).*

The Holy Liturgy itself reminds us of the whole life of the Lord, His death for us and His second coming to judge the world. It reminds us to wait for His coming and prepare ourselves. It also reminds us to be spiritually prepared to partake of His Divine Sacraments which give us life.

Some Benefits Of Remembrance

Remembrance helps us not to sin. After the fall of man in the Garden of Eden, the Lord made a remembrance for Adam, Eve and their offspring to help them not to sin in that He pronounced a punishment for their disobedience. The punishment for Adam is that he will eat his bread by the sweat of his face and for Eve that she brings forth Children in pain (Gen. 3:19,16). Although God provided a perfect redemption for the disobedience of man He still pronounced these punishments as a reminder for us not to be disobedient again.

God preserved this punishment after redemption had taken place so that by remembering, we may be humbled and repent.

God's love can forgive everything but punishment is necessary for us so that we may not forget that sin is very bad and there is condemnation.

So, it is improper for us to complain of punishment but rather we should benefit from it spiritually.

Remembrance of sins is useful, as David the Prophet says, *"My sin is ever before me…" (Ps.51:3).*

We remember our sins in order to repent and be ashamed of them. It also helps us not to become proud. Therefore St. Paul the Apostle did not forget that he persecuted the church, even after his ascension to the third heaven and said, *"I am not worthy to be called an apostle, because I persecuted the church of God." (1 Cor: 15:9).*

Why also should we not forget our sins?

We should not forget them so that we may have compassion upon those who fall (Hab.13:3) and also that we may be on guard not to fall again. We should remember our sins so that God might forgive them for us.

St Anthony the Great says concerning this, *"If we forget our sins, God would remember them against us, but if we remember our sins, God would forget them for us."*

Do not say then, *'Since God has forgiven my sins, let me forget them. They are obliterated!'* You are not better than David the Prophet or Paul the Apostle, who remembered their sins after they had been forgiven.

As well as not forgetting your sins, you should not forget God's loving kindnesses towards you because by forgetting you neglect to give thanks and your love for God will grow cold.

These two matters are seriously dangerous for your spiritual life!!

The Lord ordered the people to set up stones for remembrance so that they might not forget their crossing the Jordan (Josh.4:9). Daily we remember the event of the crossing of the Red Sea in the midnight Psalmody. The Manna and the rod of Aaron that had sprouted and were put in the Ark of Testimony as a memorial.

Remember Gods' loving kindnesses and remember your promises and vows to God. This will be useful for your spirituality.

Remember all your promises to God when you were in trouble and when He covered your sins. Remember what you promised Him in every confession and in every Holy communion and be ashamed of what you do after this.

The holy people did not forget at all Gods' loving kindnesses towards them.

If you put God's love before you, His love will be kindled in your heart.

The church set the thanksgiving prayer as an introduction for every prayer so that we may not forget God's loving kindness. You can add to it your own prayers so that you express your love of God and be ashamed of His love to you. These acts and prayers will help you not to sin.

Also do not forget God's promises or His care so that you don't suffer fear or anxiety.

Whenever a trouble befalls you, remember that God is your father and that He preserves and cares for you, Remember His words, *"No man shall be able to stand before you all the days of your life... I will not leave you nor forsake you…" (Josh.1:5), "I am. with you, and no one will attack you to hurt you." (Acts 18:10),* ". A *thousand may fall at your side, and ten thousand at your right hand,· But it shall not come near you." (Ps. 91:7).*

He who gets afraid and anxious is a person who forgets God's love and promises.

Even when one forgets, one must say to God along with David the Prophet, *"Remember the word to Your servant, upon which You have caused me to hope. This is my comfort in my affliction." (Ps. 119:49,50).*

All these will protect you from being anxious at the time of temptation. So, learn by heart the verses which give you hope and confidence in God's work for you and give you deep faith. Put them always in your mind and recite them often so that you may not forget them and so that you may have comfort and rejoice in the Lord.

There is another thing which you must never forget:

Remember Your Sojourning On Earth

David the Prophet used to contemplate on this matter continuously saying in his prayers, *"I am a stranger in the earth; do not hide Your commandments from me" (Ps.119:19), "I am a stranger with You, a sojourner, as all my fathers were." (Ps39:12).*

The feeling of being a stranger reminded David of death and he took benefit from its remembrance. So, David said, *"Lord, make me to know my end, and what is the measure of my days, that I may know how frail I am." (Ps.39:4).*

This was not the feeling of David the Prophet only but of all the other fathers as St. Paul the Apostle said about them, *"These all...confessed that they were strangers and pilgrims on the earth... But now they desire a better that is, a heavenly country,..."(Heb. 11:13,16).*

Remembrance of eternity prevents one from sinning, so all the holy fathers and anchorites remembered death and had their day of departure always before them.

The last point is:

Remember Your Weakness

When you remember your weakness, you will keep away from the atmosphere of sin and other offences. You will also be on your guard and be strict in your life and so will succeed in your spiritual struggle.

Those who boasted fell.

It is said of sin that it, *"...has cast down many wounded, And all who were slain by (her) were strong." (Prov.7:26).*

But those who are aware of their own weakness, are humble and humility is a strong weapon feared by the devils. A humble person prays asking for God's help and will therefore conquer. Knowing this, be not forgetful but rather benefit from it.

For example, forget the ill-treatment of others, forget the good works you have done, forget the vain worldly matters and forget all the fears which the enemy frightens you with.

A Question

Some may state that when they put their sins before them all the time (Ps. 51) they fall in them again! Of course, what is meant by remembrance of sins is not remembrance of the offending details which may cause one to be affected and to fall.

But now I refer you to the chapter entitled 'War of Thoughts' for a detailed answer.

CHAPTER 5

DOUBT

Doubt And Its Harms

Doubt is a result of weak faith and a lack of steadfastness. The Lord said to St Peter, *"O you of little faith, why did you doubt?"* (Matt. 14:31). It is also a state of unclear vision or confusion.

Doubt is torment for both the mind and heart. It may easily enter into oneself but can hardly be removed. It may leave a hidden effect which appears afterwards.

Doubt makes a person lose their peace and their comfort. Miracles may not take place because of doubt, but they happen to the simple people who believe.

If doubt lasts, it may turn into a disease or create a number of undesirable outcomes.

Doubt may destroy one's nerves and cause one to lose sleep from the anxiety it brings. It also results in hesitation, lack of confidence and being indecisive.

Kinds Of Doubt

Some examples of doubt are, doubt concerning faith, God and dogma, doubt concerning people and friends, doubt concerning oneself, concerning virtues, concerning the possibility or acceptance of repentance and doubt concerning ministry and manner of life.

1. Doubt concerning God.

Doubt concerning God's existence is an intellectual war waged by the devil.

It may be due to books and atheist views or to the company of atheists and discussing matters beyond one's understanding. This war may come also through conflicting research in the fields of philosophy, sciences or the history of the universe and its origin.

God's existence may be argued by people in order to draw attention to themselves.

Doubt may not arise concerning Gods' existence but instead concerning His help and protection, His love and true promises or concerning the benefit of prayers.

When Rebecca doubted God's promises concerning Jacob gaining Isaac's blessing, she acted in a wrong way deceiving Isaac (Gen. 27).

And when Abraham the Patriarch doubted God's promises as to giving him offspring as the stars of heaven and the sand of the sea, he behaved also in an impulsive way (Gen. 16).

2. Doubts concerning dogma.

It may be the result of being affected by the views of other sects due to attending their meetings or reading their books and pamphlets, especially when the persons' faith is weak. For example a person may attend the meetings of the Adventist's or receive preachers from Jehovah's Witnesses or be influenced by non-Orthodox articles or sermons. Hence, doubt enters into the heart and mind of such a person. A person ought to be firm in their faith. See how beautiful are the words of the Apostle, *"...always be ready to give a defense to everyone who asks you a reason for the hope that is in you..."* (*1Pet.3:15*).

A person needs to be firm with respect to his belief, as if built on rock. Some may try to convince you that the study of dogma is hard and void of spirituality but without this study you could easily doubt your faith when asked difficult question. But I advise you to read spiritual books and books on dogma and theology as well.

3. Doubt concerning friends.

This doubt is due to a lack of confidence or love of your friends; because when one loves some person truly, they will have confidence in them and thereupon will not doubt. The remedy in this case is speaking frankly, face to face and lovingly.

A person must not be affected by things heard or by slander and must not believe everything said, for accusation is often oppressive in spite of the obvious proofs given! You must not condemn anyone hastily or without hearing from them.

4. Doubt concerning people.

You may attribute a single persons fault to all who are affiliated to them whether it be a family, corporation, religion, suburb, city or country. For example, the fault of one member of a family raises doubts against the whole family, though some of its members may be righteous.

5. Doubt concerning virtues.

Someone may fill you with doubt by stating, *'What is the necessity of fasting? Is bodily virtue of any value? What is the use of abstinence? What is the necessity of chastity or prayers since God cares for us whether we pray or not?'*

Such a person may go as far as to say to you, *'What is the necessity of virtues? They are mere works, or law! And you know that man is not justified by law!!'*

They may also say, *'Do whatever you like as long as you believe and you will not perish! Even if you fall seven times you will surely rise again!'*

Doubt may extend to principles and morals, to what is allowed and what is forbidden.

Doubt may be concerning modern inventions such as television, radio, cinema and music; whether they are allowed or forbidden. It may be concerning many things new to the society such as birth control and artificial insemination etc.

It depends on the spirit not on letter, and on understanding and study.

For example, is it right or wrong to watch a movie in the cinema? This depends on the movie and your intention in going. The same may be said of T.V, radio, video, internet, music and acting, are they used for good or evil?

6. Doubt concerning oneself.

Sometimes a person doubts themselves, loses self-confidence and have no trust in their own powers and abilities! An example of this is, a student who doubts their ability to succeed or doubts the sufficiency of time given for an exam. Or a person who doubts their own behaviour whether it is right or wrong! Or whether they are loved or hated by people.

This happens to children, so we give a child self-confidence by praising and encouraging them.

But cruel treatment and over correcting a person may lead to personality disorders and always doubting oneself.

Even adults need encouragement and kind words. They need to be cheered up especially in times of illness, when they are facing a problem or a tribulation. This encouragement will prevent them from falling into despair.

Here, a person doubts what fate awaits them.

A person may also have doubts concerning their manner of living; what suits them or what is proper for them?

Does marriage or the life of celibacy suit them? A life of monasticism, ministry or consecration? Would they succeed in this or not? Would they be firm in their choice or regret it? Is a certain study or job suitable for them or not?

These may be mere questions or may become doubts which trouble and confuse a person. They may lead a person to be hesitant, so they become unable to decide. Doubt continues with such a person even though they consult others or cast lots.

Doubts may stand in the way of some people when taking important decisions. Their way may become unclear and they hesitate to commit.

One must be sure of the goal of their spiritual life. One must also examine oneself for their attributes and abilities so that you may know your weaknesses.

As to doubt concerning one's power, the words of St. Paul the Apostle give comfort, *"I can do all things through Christ who strengthens me." (Phil.4:13).*

7. Doubt concerning ministry.

A minister often doubts the success of their ministry, whether they ought to continue or to stop. This may be caused by wanting immediate results and if they don't get the results that they want, they doubt the success of their ministry.

Ministry is like agriculture; a seed needs time to grow and establish roots in the ground, similarly the results of ministry may take time to manifest.

St. Augustine's mother continued in long prayers for him during which time no fruit appeared but she did not give up or doubt in God's grace.

Reasons For Doubt

They may be internal, coming from oneself, or external. We shall contemplate on all reasons in order to reach a suitable remedy.

1. Doubt may be due to one's own nature.

For example, a person with a weak personality or someone who has personality problems may be inclined to easily doubt. People who are narrow-minded also seem to have problems trusting. If they were broad-minded, their doubts would vanish.

2. Simplicity and depth.

A simple person believes everything that is said to them and finds no reason to doubt. For example, someone will tell a simple-minded person that their friend is critical of them and they believe them and become upset with their friend.

A simple person may have doubts when they are deceived by people concerning faith or dogma.

Through critical thinking we may discover these seeds of doubt and avoid them.

But sometimes critical thinking may lead one to a kind of philosophy through which they lose simplicity of heart. They long to comprehend theological or spiritual mysteries with their limited minds and so develop doubts. This is the reason why philosophers often fall into doubts.

3. Fear.

Fear and doubt are often inseparable. Each of them may be the cause or the result of the other.

Fear leads to doubt, and doubt causes fear.

When St. Peter walked on water and doubted, doubt caused him to fear; and when he feared his doubts increased and he fell into the water and cried out.

4. Diabolic wars.

Doubt is very often a war from the devil, it is an old war, an example of which is his leading our forefathers to doubt the nature of the forbidden tree and doubt the result of eating of it. This made them doubt God's commandment to them.

The devil tried to tempt the Lord on the mountain using doubt but he failed. Similarly on the cross he addressed the Lord saying through others, *"If You are the Son of God, come down from the cross..." (Matt.27:40).* Through doubt, the devil tried to dissuade St. Anthony from monasticism.

The devil may even bring doubts to a person at the hour of their death to make them perish.

The devil has many thousands of years of experience attacking the human race and as such has many ways that he can bring doubt into our hearts.

He plants doubts concerning our faith and our relationships with others. He does this to confuse and embarrass us.

Doubts do not come from the devil only but also from...

5. The Environment.

Mary Magdalene who saw the Lord Jesus Christ after the resurrection and He spoke to her, doubted His resurrection when she found herself amidst suspicions and slanders which were spread everywhere by the Jews! (John 20).

Doubts may also come from the company of the doubtful. As faith and trust are transferred to you through the company of confident believers, doubt also is transferred through the company of the doubtful. So, keep away from the company of those or at least be aware of their talk and do not believe everything that they try and persuade you off.

Similarly reading materials that arouse inner doubt. Avoid reading such material and choose books that build you rather than destroy your belief and morals!

Some writers like to raise doubts within the reader against firm axioms in order to appear that they understand what others don't!

Other sources of doubt are gossips and rumours, which are often wrong. So, do not believe whatever is said and do not repeat rumours yourself.

6. Jumping to conclusions.

Some examples of this are:

-A friend does not attend a party which you invited them to and although there may be many reasons why, you choose to explain it that they don't like you. So you have planted doubt in your friendship.

- A wife may imagine only one explanation why her husband returns home late after work and this would cause her to doubt her husband's fidelity.

An amazing observation to note is that those who confine themselves to only one explanation, usually choose the worst one, the one that troubles them and confuses their thoughts.

-Another example is the daughter who returns home late. The parents may jump to the worst possible conclusions, like she had an accident, or she has been kidnapped or any other evil may have befallen her. They become anxious till the daughter returns and perhaps they may doubt whether she will return at all!

7. Delay.

-As in the case of our father Abraham who did not have any offspring for a long time.

Or people who suffer a certain trial or problem for a long time without it being solved.

8. Doubt due to troubles.

We have as an example from the story of Gideon in the Old Testament when he asked the angel, *"If the Lord is with us, why then has all this happened to us? And where are all His miracles which our fathers told us about? (Judges 6:13).*

Another example is the doubts of the people of Israel in the wilderness in front of the Red Sea (Exod.14).

Great danger may make a person fall into doubt. This happened to the Israelite army before Goliath the Giant, unlike David the Prophet who had no doubts at all but addressed the giant in confidence saying, *"This day the Lord will deliver you into my hand…" (I Sam. 17:46)*.

When troubles continue for a long time, one may suffer despair and doubt God's mercy. In their doubt they may think some sorcery is used against them and in their despair, they may resort to sorcery to stop its effect!

Troubles and delay require a strong heart that is not affected by doubts.

9. Generalization of faults.

For example, a girl living in a house where the parents are always quarreling becomes afraid of marriage imagining that if she gets married, the same thing will happen to her. She has doubts regarding all potential suitors that he will treat her as her father treated her mother!

Or a person who tells their friend a secret but the friend discloses it. So, they doubt all their friends and doubt in their sincerity. They may become self-centered and not tell a secret to anyone, even the nearest to their heart saying to themselves that they may do the same thing!

A person may think that the people of a certain country are all misers and they advise not to marry a person from that country.

This idea is implanted within them because of an individual event.

+ Doubt Due To Delusions/Superstitions

A person may imagine that number thirteen conceals something evil behind it. So, they feel doubtful about every day which carries the number 13 or its multiplications whether in the Gregorian, the Arabic or Coptic month.

They doubt if the number of their house is 13 or their telephone number includes 13 or the application for a job carries that number. The idea may be magnified within their mind and they become mistrustful.

It may be hard to remove this belief out of their mind.

CHAPTER 6

FEAR

Two General Assumptions

With regards to fear, we must keep in mind two important assumptions:

1. Not all fear is sin or a spiritual war because there is holy fear.

2. Fear did not exist in human nature at the time of creation, before the sin of our forefathers.

When God created Adam, he lived with the beasts without any fear and his relation with God was also void of fear.

After sinning, Adam began to be afraid and because of his exceeding fear he hid behind the trees and said to God, *"I heard Your voice in the garden, and I was afraid..." (Gen.3:10)*.

The disease of fear increased since Cain killed his brother and it turned into terror. We hear Cain saying to God, *"Surely You have driven me out this day from the face of the ground; I shall be hidden from Your face; I shall be a fugitive and a vagabond on the earth, and it will happen that anyone who finds me will kill me." (Gen. 4:14)*.

Since then, fear became a psychological disease and entered into the nature of man.

There appeared various reasons and results for fear, and it became a spiritual war used by the devil for fighting man.

There came to be degrees of fear, dread, cowardice fright, dismay and terror. A person may even die of strong fear or may lose their mind. Their nerves may collapse and their body tremble out of fear.

Holy Fear

It is the kind of fear meant by the words, *"The fear of the Lord is the beginning of wisdom." (Ps.111:10, Prove. 9:10)*. Also, *"Conduct yourselves throughout the time of your sojourning here in fear…" (1 Pet 1:17)*.

The Lord Jesus Christ says also, *"And do not fear those who kill the body but cannot kill the soul. But rather fear Him who is able to destroy both soul and body in hell." (Matt. 10:28), "…yes, I say to you, fear Him." (Luke 12:5)*.

Here the Lord Jesus Christ presents to us two kinds of fear; one required and the other wrong.

God's fear leads to awe and obedience to Him. It leads to keeping His commandments, loving Him and leads to a life of repentance and sincerity.

However, holy fear is not the subject of our talk today rather we want to concentrate here on spiritual wars.

Natural Fear

A psychologist said that fear is due to three causes; darkness, the unknown, and sudden movement.

It is evident that the three of them fall under one cause i.e. the unknown; for darkness conceals behind it something unknown and a sudden movement is due to a unknown reason.

113

Yet, there are some persons who are bold, who do not fear darkness nor sudden movement but in spite of this, they are not spiritual.

Fear Of Death

Most people fear harm and fear death. They also fear what happens after death. It is very rare to find a person who does not fear death. This kind of fear may also be fear of the unknown.

Death is an unknown. What is beyond death is also unknown.

A person fears death because they do not know how they would die and how theirs soul would leave their body. All these matters frighten many people.

On the other hand a person who is sure of their destiny after death, has no fear of it but longs for it.

Hence, St. Paul the Apostle says, "... *having a desire to depart and be with Christ, which is far better." (Phil. 1:23).* No doubt also the thief on the right hand of the Lord was not afraid of death after he had heard the promise, "*...today you will be with Me in Paradise." (Luke 23. 43).*

Neither was Simeon the Elder afraid of death because he demanded it from the Lord saying, *"Lord, now let Your servant depart in peace, according to Your word; for my eyes have seen Your salvation..." (Luke 2:29,30).*

Those who fears death are the unrepentant and unprepared

for it and also those who love the present world.

All this reveals a sin. Though fear of death is something natural, the reasons leading to fear here are sin.

Some of the saints who were known for their humility were afraid of death because they felt they were sinners.

Fear of death either makes one get ready for it or flee from it.

A spiritual person prepares for death through repentance and love of God. This preparation causes fear to disappear and God gives them peace.

But the devil may use the fear of death to make a person flee from it. They are uncomfortable at any talk about death or any news concerning it. They will indulge in the pleasures of this life to avoid this troublesome subject!

It is a pity that relatives and physicians of a sick person, whose condition is critical and approaching death, avoid mentioning that fearful name 'death', in front of them. They lie to them and calm them falsely, engaging them in worldly and unprofitable conversation in order to make them forget that they are dying. They relieve them of the fear of death until it befalls them suddenly when they are not ready for it.

The devil may also tempt his victim saying, 'Since you will die, enjoy life to the full'. This was the idea of the Epicureans, *"...Let us eat and drink, for tomorrow we die."* (*1Cor. 15:32*).

Hence we see that fear of death is one weapon and avoiding the fear of death is another weapon.

The devil fights with both but when he finds that a person has become sure of their death, the devil fights them with another method to prevent them from repenting and from getting ready for death; he makes the fear of death paralyze their mind and confines them in this fear so that it consumes them and they become unable to properly prepare for eternity. He puts before them only the sorrows and pains of death so they neglect to think of eternity and preparing for it.

In other cases, the devil may use the fear of death to throw a person into deadly sins such as denying their faith.

Here, we state that the martyrs and confessors never feared death but rather longed for it to attain a better life and the company of God, His angles and His saints.

Love of eternity relieves the heart from the fear of death and gives it a spirit that is always prepared.

Eternity, the heavenly Jerusalem, the glorified resurrection and life in spirit are beautiful subjects which Gods' children need to contemplate. They ought to let their influence go deep into their hearts, their thoughts and their feelings.

Whoever fears death, fears also its causes such as sicknesses.

A person who fears sicknesses, may also try to protect themselves against it in an excessive way that is based on paranoid fear which doubts everything.

The devil may use the fear of sicknesses to throw a person into worldly pleasures. He encourages them to eat and drink and take vitamins to improve their health; to practice sports or have recreation, to think of nothing stressful or disturbing, to do little work, to reduce their activities, their labour and their effort. They do all or any of this in an exaggerated and very frightened way. The devil does this to make the person neglect important spiritualities and their duties to others. Their health becomes their only goal.

However, illness is not the only cause for death. Some may die due to courage and bravery such as soldiers.

If fear of death creeps into the heart of a person, it robs them of their courage and bravery and changes them into a coward who is weak in spirit and deprives them of any good personal qualities So the words of St. Augustine in this respect prove true, for he says, '*I sat on the top of the world, when felt within me that I feared nothing and desired nothing.*'

This leads us to another point concerning fear.

Fear Of People

It is another spiritual war which attacks those having a weak soul. These types of people may not fear God as much as they fear people and dread their harm!! They imagine that people are powerful enough to make an assault upon them, or destroy their career, or cause them trouble or harm, or defame them or resist their hopes. So, they give much consideration to them.

The devil benefits from this fear, making the fearful person use false or exaggerated flattery, hypocrisy or the like to the person they fear. They think that they can gain the love and approval of them or at least avoid their harm. Thus they become of no value in the eyes of others and are debased. In order to please people, they are ready to call evil good and good evil and be enemies of the enemies of those people and friends to their friends!! Hence their principles and morals are lost and perhaps their faith also would be lost!! A person may also betray their beloved due to fear.

In such a case one forgets the words of the Holy Bible; *"We ought to obey God rather than men." (Acts 5:29), "He who justifies the wicked, and he who condemns the just, both of them alike are an abomination to the Lord." (Prov. 17:15).* The only concern of that person becomes how to be saved from the one they fear, no matter how wrong or troublesome for the conscience the means may be.

Through fear and a mean spirit, one remembers only certain sayings such as;' Please them since you are on their land; cover their faults since you are in their house; Salute them since you are in their district.'*

(*The words in Arabic rhyme and they mean approving of others' behaviour even though it may be wrong.)

They do whatever they do and say whatever they say. They are ready to change according to circumstances.

Fear carries such a person with the current. They are led by fear not by conscience.

If you blame such a person and remind them of spiritual principles, they will answer, 'what shall I do? My life is in the hands of those people!' If you say to them that their life is in the hands of God alone, you seem to be speaking theoretically not of matters of fact and practice.

Truly, many are those whom the devil destroyed with fear whose inner faith was much less than their outer fears.

Many worshipped human beings rather than God, not only out of fear they would harm them but also out of fear of losing privileges or worldly gains that they provide! A person who is controlled by their earthly desires, fears to lose them and so 'goes with the flow', pleases people.

Such persons did not fear only their superiors at work, or those who are a source of their gains but also those who are the source of their pleasures!!

Here we observe many faults of these fearful persons; love of pleasure, fear of losing such, flattering those who are able to deprive them of such pleasure, their continued fear in order to continue in pleasure and so on.

Some may fear those who can reveal their faults. They may either dread them and hence try to please them so they keep their mouths shut or in an extreme circumstance, the devil may lead them to get rid of them by committing some crime!

For example, a thief may kill the person who sees him steal; an adulterer may kill the person who reveals his sin etc. The murderer in such cases in not powerful but on the contrary, they are weak and afraid.

People in general fear those who are more powerful than them, whether in intellect or physically or in capability.

When an adversary senses that you fear them, that makes them more confident to attack or take advantage of you. They feel that you are not able to resist them, so they attack or continue frightening you. You, out of fear, submit more to them and by being at their mercy you are exposed to more harm…., you are now trapped in this vicious circle.

The devil deals with people in the same way as we shall see in the next point.

Fear Of The Devil

The devil rejoices to see you afraid of him, for when you are afraid you submit to him or get desperate of fighting and stop resisting him. You may also feel defeated in every war with him and so you don't put up much resistance to him, struggling bravely. The Apostle says about this, *"Resist him, steadfast in the faith…"* (*1Pet.5:9*). You should do this even though the devil is like a roaring lion (1Pet.5:8).

St. Anthony was not afraid of the devil when he fought him using many varying methods, even when he appeared to him in terrifying forms. St. Anthony did not fear to spend the night in a tomb amidst corpses (Paradise of the Holy Father Vol. 1).

Also St. Macarius the Great was not afraid of the devil, he even once used a human skull as a pillow for his head. The devil seeing how bold he was tried to scare him by speaking through the skull but he was not moved and at all and rebuked them (Paradise of the Holy Father Vol. 1).

Our fathers conquered the devil because they did not fear him and because God gave them, as He gives us, power over all the devils.

How beautiful are the words of our Lord Jesus Christ, *"I saw Satan fall like lightning from heaven." (Luke 10:18).*

Do not be afraid then of the devils because you have the divine power that is much greater than the power with which they fight you.

Do not be afraid also because God, *"...will not allow you to be tempted beyond what you are able." (1Cor.10:13).*

The devil cannot touch you without God's permission. This is best illustrated in the story of Job the just. God allows the devil only to tempt you within the scope of your abilities to overcome him.

Do not give the devil then more ability than be really has and do not fear him more than you ought to. Know that you only have to be on your guard against him.

This leads us to another issue!

Fear Without A Cause

Many are afraid for no serious reason. Theirs is either childish fear or a disease. A child imagines thieves or ghosts in the house and so is afraid, while there is nothing.

Grown-ups also may be afraid of things which do not exist or suspect imaginary fears which do not exist at all but are created by their imagination!

There are psychological diseases of this kind like the fear complex which makes a sick person imagine that there are persons trying to harm them.

Fear may also be due to the work of the devils who fill them with fear or implant non-existent suspicions in their minds. They may suggest that there is someone who is plotting against them, who follows them or tries to do them harm.

The Remedy

One needs to remember God's promises which say to us, *"Do not be afraid....for I am with you, and no one will attack you to hurt you.." (Acts 18:10);* and remember also God's protection and help.

Faith removes fear and reminds a frightened person of the divine power preserving them.

How beautiful are the words of David the prophet, *"Yea, though I walk through the valley of the shadow of death; I will fear no evil; for You are with me." (Ps.23:4).*

CHAPTER 7

WAR OF THOUGHTS

Wrong Thoughts

A person ought to live pure in spirit, body, soul, mind and feelings and in everything... We pray to God in the holy liturgy saying, *'Every thought that displeases Your goodness, may it be cast away from us'.*

We also say in our Agbia prayers, *'Purify our souls, our bodies, our spirits, our thoughts and our intentions.'* Thoughts then need purification.

Wrong thoughts which pass through the mind may be thoughts of anger, revenge, haughtiness, pride, vain glory, day dreams, thoughts of envy, jealousy, worldly lusts, thoughts of adultery and uncleanliness... and so on. Hence we ask in the holy liturgy to be purified of *'...the memory of evil that entails death'.*

Since all evil leads to spiritual death, we must not let its memory into our minds.

Avoiding The Memory Of Evil

Remembering the sins of others may make you fall into condemnation or scorning or judging them. Remembering the offences of people against you may make you hate them, be angry towards them and desire revenge. While remembering bodily sins may defile your mind and lead you again to carnal lusts.

Continuous remembrance of evil fixes it within one's self and one's unconscious mind. From such wrong remembrances come evil thoughts, evil suspicions, doubts and also lusts. Sins may also appear in the form of dreams.

So, reject all evil thoughts and do not try to engage them. Even if you recall the evil out of regret it may still harm you. For how do you know what may happen? The thought may enter into your mind through regret and then turns into an internal war. In this case evil scenes would return to your mind not with the purpose of repenting of them but in the form of passion and lust.

One may ask, 'Shall I not put my sin before me and rebuke myself for it in order to repent and be humbled?'. I say, 'You can remember your sin in general but beware of indulging in offensive or exciting details'!

This concerns mainly sins of passion and lust, especially if the person has not got rid of them completely nor attained complete chastity because they may fight him again. If you begin to remember the details of such sins, you will lead yourself into their sphere once more.

Rebuking oneself for a sin may be a mere deceit used by the devil to let a thought into your mind. The devil may take such a holy chance (of rebuking oneself) to make one deviate into an opposite direction.

The Beginning Of The Thought

A sinful thought may not begin as a sinful thought, otherwise it would be too obvious and a person with a pure heart would flee from it, dismiss it or resist it by any means lest it should settle. It may begin in a deceitful form, perhaps as holy zeal and a desire to build God's Kingdom. In their holy zeal they study and become critical of things which need to be reformed. They then begin to judge and be critical of the people who are working or responsible in those areas that need to be reformed. In doing this reform they may resort to cruelty and rage, condemning people and or dismissing them. It ends with hatred and enmity and only then does the person realize that their initial thought was sinful.

A thought may begin in a different way, such as showing compassion towards those who fall and trying to save them. In helping them they get deeply involved discussing every detail and become totally absorbed in any news or information. It ends by them falling into the same fault, at least in their thoughts. So, we say that not every person is fit for saving others or for attempts of reformation.

A sinful thought may begin weak.

In such a form, you imagine that you can overcome it easily but the more you keep it within you and argue with it, the more it becomes firm and dominates over you. That is because you gave it the opportunity to enter into the fortress of your thoughts. By keeping the thought within you means that you want it and since you want it, you will be unable to dismiss it. Also keeping the thought makes it persist and exert pressure on your feelings and here you may become weak before it. Hence you will no longer have the power required to dismiss it or will required greater will-power to overcome it. Truly it would have been easier to dismiss the thought immediately!!

When the thought from the serpent to Eve began it was weak, a mere question. She was actually able to refute it strongly. She mentioned that God did not only say "'You shall not eat it,...but also "...nor shall you touch it,.." (Gen. 3:3).

But when Eve entertained the sinful thought and was exposed to its continuous suggestions and enticements, she began to get weaker. The thought within her turned into doubt and desire; then at last she stretched out her hand and ate. She fell and made others fall.

The same thing happened to Cain.

God told him that sin lay at the door; it didn't enter yet and that he (Cain) should rule over it (Gen. 4:7). However, as the thought pressed him, he let it into his heart and argued with it, he submitted at last and the thought took hold of him and led him to kill his brother.

By not dismissing a sinful thought quickly you betray the Lord and as a result His grace forsakes you and you become vulnerable to falling as the thought has power over you.

Grace may forsake you also because by keeping the thought within you could be due to pride or self-confidence. You convince yourself that you are stronger than the thought and that you can dismiss it at any moment if you want!! So, grace forsakes you to make you aware of your weakness.

So in future flee immediately from any sinful thought and in this act of humility you will overcome it

Another reason the weak thought which entered your mind was able to overcome you is that you may be fighting alone; you did not ask God in prayer to save you from it; you forget to cross yourself with the sign of the cross, which is an act that shows you need power from on high.

Sources Of A Sinful Thought

1. A thought may come from a previous train of thought.

Thoughts are not barren but they bring forth thoughts of their own kind. There may be a thought which began some days before and wants to be completed, or a story which began but did not end and requires more details even out of curiosity. Flee from such matters.

2. A sinful thought may come from a certain experience.

3. From some stories, feelings or desires which settled within your unconscious mind and appear in your conscious mind and argue with you!

So, be careful to keep your unconscious mind pure and do not store in it anything which may disturb the purity of your mind. If there are old sins or offences stored in it, do not use them and they will be removed with the passage of time and by neglecting them. If you do this, new pure thoughts will replace them within you.

4. The unconscious mind stores thoughts from various sources such as things read or heard, scenes, ideas and desires.

Be careful then to keep your heart pure while reading, hearing, seeing or thinking. Let your desires also be pure and your senses as well, for St. Isaac says, 'Senses are the gates of thoughts' and this is our next point.

5. Senses are the gates of thought.

Beware of the senses which "..*go to and fro on earth and walk back and forth on it.*" *(Job 1:7)*. They wander here and there bringing into the mind thoughts from rash impure looks, bad things heard and from whatever things smelt or touched.

Pure senses bring pure thoughts, while defiled senses bring defiled thoughts; also rash senses bring rash thoughts.

No doubt restraining senses helps to restrain thoughts as well. He who attains purity of mind has also to watch his senses and train them to have spiritual caution.

6. A sinful thought may also come from the devil or from people. Solomon who was the wisest on earth was in due time influenced by his wives (1 Kings 11:3).

Many husbands failed in their married life because of the nagging of his mother or sister concerning his wife. He was influenced and new thoughts entered into his mind which did not exist before during the engagement period or the first months of marriage. Many wives also failed because of the advice given them by their families.

Strange thoughts come to a person from outside sources which can change his nature and character.

So, check your thoughts continually and do not be under the influence or domination of any person, holding their views without examining them. This may happen in the case of some spiritual guides or teachers.

Often a person who admires a leader or influential figure wants to copy them, they become carbon copies of them repeating their words and thinking their thoughts holding all their views however wrong or sinful they may be.

7. Thoughts may come from the devil which he plants in the mind. They may be merely a suggestion.

A person must discern whether a thought is from God or from the devil. If a person has not the gift of discernment, they can consult whoever has such a gift.

The devil does not compel a person to accept his thoughts, he just entices the person through suggestions He did this with our forefathers Adam and Eve.

A spiritual person has to resist every thought which contradicts God's commandment as the Apostle says, *"Resist him steadfast in the faith..." (1 Pet 5:9).*

Here, I state an important rule and it's our next point.

War And Falling

Not every sinful thought which comes to one's mind is sin. It may be merely a war and there is a difference between a war and a fall.

In a spiritual war, there are sinful thoughts which press hard on the mind, perhaps for a long time and though a person refuses them and resists with all his power, they continue.

As for falling through thoughts, it means that a person accepts a thought and does not resist it or resists it in a formal weak way which expresses in fact submission and satisfaction!!

Acceptance of a sinful thought is betrayal of God because one opens the gates of the heart to God's enemies and accepts them in place of God. In such a case, a person defiles their own holy temple, which is in fact the temple of the Holy Spirit (I Cor. 3:16). When this is done it is as if you are dismissing the Spirit of God from your heart because, *"What communion has light with darkness." (2Cor. 6:14)*.

In the case of falling through thought, a person finds pleasure in the thought, justifies it, develops and encourages it, keeps it and adds to it.

A person becomes united with the thought and becomes one spirit with it. During that time, they cannot distinguish between the thought which began as a war and the thought coming out of themselves, from their own heart and mind!

The thought causing the fall may be the result of some lust or desire. Lusts and thoughts replace each other as cause and result.

A sinful thought results in lust and lust leads to sinful thought.

Each is either a cause or a result of the other; both strengthen each other for the same goal. In such a case, the external thought co-operates with the internal thought.

Things Which Lead To Falling

There are other things which lead to falling through thought such as relaxation, idleness, weakness, submission, love of telling stories and desires.

1. When a person is fought with a sinful thought but remains idle and relaxing, the thought will get harder and may have power to make him fall easily.

In the case of being idle, a thought finds the person alone without any resistance or defense.

There is a saying which says, 'The mind of the lazy is a laboratory for the devil.' The Holy Bible says that the devil comes and if he finds the person idle and lazy, *"...then he goes and takes with him seven other spirits more wicked than himself, and they enter and dwell there." (Luke 11:24,25).*

So, in your time of leisure, be on guard against any thoughts which may come to you. It is better not to leave your mind empty.

The nature of the mind is to work all the time. It is always engaged either in important matters or trivial matters but it does not stop.

2. When relaxing, the mind thinks of any matter, and may think of various tales, news and thoughts. Here, the enemy may take the chance and throw into this mind a sinful thought or a thought which leads to sin without its being aware. Here, one must be alert and dismiss that thought quickly before it settles and continues.

It is better in the case of relaxation, to engage yourself in some calm simple thing which does not lead to sin.

Relaxation, in fact, means relieving the nerves not throwing oneself into thoughts.

3. Spiritual weakness also leads to the fall through thoughts because in such a case one cannot resist but submits to thoughts.

So, when a spiritual person finds themselves weak, they have to be more careful and more aware: They have to be alert and provide themselves with all the spiritual nourishment necessary to strengthen themselves, in order to overcome their weakness.

Beware of all conditions of weakness and escape during such times from all causes of offences and thoughts.

Perhaps the Lord meant such conditions when He said, *"And pray that your flight may not be in winter or on the Sabbath." (Matt. 24:20).*

"In winter" symbolically refers to the time of spiritual coldness where there is no fervor. "On the Sabbath" refers to the time of rest and relaxation. Both matters are dangerous but…..

4. Do not submit however weak you are.

Be steadfast in fighting the adversary until you gain power from on high which would deliver you and rebuke the devil on your behalf.

This is what happened to Joshua the high priest concerning whom the Angel of the Lord said to Satan, *"The Lord rebuke you, Satan! the Lord... rebuke you! Is this not a brand plucked from the fire?" (Zech. 3:2).*

Weakness is not an excuse for falling because we can plead for help to resist the devil.

In the next article, I shall tell you how to resist a thought.

5. Do not have a love for telling sinful stories.

If you do, you will find pleasure in creating sinful stories which may injure you spiritually and satisfy your sinful desires.

In such a case, the sin is internal, coming from within you.

Many who like to invent stories either give the beginning or the devil offers them an idea and they weave from it long endless stories...

The thoughts here are mere voluntary acts which satisfy sinful desires.

Examples of such thoughts are; thoughts of revenge, fornication or day-dreams.

Kinds Of War Of Thoughts

+ Three types of people.

Three types of people are worried by thoughts:

1. Those who seek the thought.

2. Those who deal with the thought and accept it.

3. Those who have rich imagination and can create ideas and stories.

All of the three types are very much occupied by thoughts since their minds hover about certain sins because thoughts find no resistance within them but are welcomed.

1 Those who seek the thought.

Those do not wait for the thoughts to come but rather they instigate the thoughts without any resistance. They seek sources to fuel their thoughts.

Their senses are alert and searching everywhere with the intention of finding material that would fuel their minds. They rejoice in it and long for it.

These people have curiosity, they seek people's news and secrets. They find pleasure in talking about such matters and add to what they hear comments and conclusions of their own. Thus, they store in their minds images which injure them spiritually. Therefore they fall in two kinds of sins; sins of the tongue and sins of the mind. Each cause and support the other.

When a person of this type meets with some friend or acquaintance, they begin at once to ask, 'What news do you have? What has happened to so and so? What did he do? What did you see and what did you hear? What do you say of all this? What else do you know?' They go on pressing such a friend extracting all that they know as a farmer milks a cow and does not leave its udder until they extract all the milk in it. In such a way, they injure themselves and others!!

They love to know people's news and try to get some news from whomever they meet! When they sit at a table to eat with others, their eyes wander to examine what and how another eats, what they like and what they don't like! It is their way regarding every other matter even with respect to personal affairs!!

What is amazing about such a person is that whenever there is some bad news they rush to hear about it but when there is something good they are not so enthusiastic to hear it.

They collect news, secrets and thoughts; their senses are restless, tired of, "...*going to and fro on earth and walking back and forth on it.*" *(Job.2:2).*

If you ask such a person, 'What does it matter to you? what does it avail you to know all this?', you get no answer. It is a disease which turns into a habit and becomes part of their nature.

Many injured themselves and injured others because of such curiosity and their attempts to disclose secrets.

Perhaps you ask, 'What shall I do if thoughts do not come from within me but from others and I am only a victim?' I reply that you must not listen to a sinful thought or think of it, read about it or talk to anyone concerning it. You must not deal with it at all.

2. Do not deal with a thought.

Do not live with it or let it live within you but dismiss it immediately.

Do not keep the thought in your mind or even in your ears. Keep away as far as you can from those who bring you thoughts and if you are compelled to listen to them for reasons out of your control, do not pay attention. Engage yourself during such talk with something else and do not argue with them when they utter offensive words. Do not think again of any sinful talk you were compelled to hear because this fixes it in your unconscious mind. Remember always the first Psalm which commands you to avoid the path of sinners and the seat of the scornful.

So do not deal with a thought or with its causes Avoid the person who pours into your ears news that may bring thoughts or the person whose appearance, conduct or way of behavior arouses thoughts.

When David the Prophet accepted his sinful thoughts, he fell not only in the thought but into sinful actions which is worse. The same happened to Samson and many others who were strong.

Ahab the King was troubled by the thought concerning the vineyard of Naboth the Jezreelite. When the thought continued and the desire for robbing the share of others was aroused within him, his wife also adding fuel to the fire burning within him, Ahab proceeded from mere thought into murder, robbery and oppression.

So, if you are negligent in dismissing the sinful thoughts, they will bring forth other thoughts because no thought is barren.

A thought may bring forth another of its own kind or from another kind. It may also yield passion, lust or varied bad feelings or cause many countless sins which cannot be easily dismissed.

A thought becomes in this way the father of a great family of thoughts.

So, dismiss a thought from the beginning before it grows and spreads within you and before it dominates over your will. It is easy to dismiss a thought in its beginning but this becomes hard if it continues.

A sinful thought examines you first to know how pure your heart is and how ready you are within to deal with it. If you refuse to deal with it, it will know that you are not an easy person who entertains sinful thoughts, so it leaves you. If it tries to remain, it will be weak because of your inner purity.

3. Close your doors.

Beware not to open a door for thoughts.

If you open a door for some thought, this means that you begin to submit to it, to welcome it and betray your Master. You have to remember what was said about the virgin of the Song;

"A garden enclosed is my sister, my spouse, a spring shut up, a fountain sealed." (Song 4:12).

She is enclosed against any evil thought that may knock at the doors of her mind and against any sinful lust knocking at the door of her heart. She does not open to anyone. She opens the door only for chaste holy thoughts. When sinful thoughts come, that soul hears the angels singing to her;

"Praise the Lord, O Jerusalem! Praise your God, O Zion! For He has strengthened the bars of your gates. He has blessed your children within you." (Ps. 147:12,13).

Those closed gates are the gates of the virtuous soul that does not open them for every knocking thought of the enemy. She is honest to her Lord, so He blessed her children within her; those children born to her from the Holy Spirit i.e. the holy feelings.

Close your gates before the sinful thoughts because they will not stop until they are completed.

A thought is a mere obedient servant sent by lust to prepare the way for it.

It is difficult for a thought to remain idle. It develops into something more dangerous. A thought is just a step in the wars of the enemy, so be very careful lest this lead to action.

A thought develops while moving from the senses to the mind, then to the heart and then to the will.

If you keep the thought in your ears even though for a little time, it will creep into your mind where the imagination holds it and brings forth many children to it. Then the thought grows within you till it reaches your heart, your feelings, your emotions, your passions and your lusts. Here the war is at its climax.

So by dealing with a thought, it gains power over you because it has been allowed to enter within you after passing through your strongholds, it enters your city and begins mingling with its people! How dangerous this stage is for you!

For at this stage, you are fought by your own heart or in fact you are exposed to two wars, one from within and the other from without. The internal one is harder. What a thought hopes most for is to reach your heart, and there its children would gather round it against you. Its children are the lusts of the heart. When the heart falls in the hands of the thought, the will easily falls because the heart will press on it.

The will remains strong as long as the heart is strong and the thought is outside. But when the heart becomes weak, the will becomes weak accordingly. Unless Grace grants the will power from high, it will submit easily and fall in sin practically.

Therefore, close your gates from the beginning so that you may not proceed into dangerous stages.

St. Dorotheos says, *'It is easy to pull out a small herb but if you neglect it till it becomes a huge oak, you will find it difficult to pull out.'*

So, pull out the thoughts from the first step and hearken to the beautiful words of the Psalm, *"Happy shall he be who takes and dashes your little ones against the rock." (Ps.137:9).* This means to take the sins when they are still small i.e. mere thoughts before they grow and dashes them against the rock *"...and the Rock was Christ..." (1 Cor.10:4).*

The Harm Of Retaining Thoughts

As we have said, if one does not dismiss the thought immediately, it will gain power over one and settle within. It will also reach the heart and the will; it will trouble the soul and bring forth other thoughts and sins.

Even though a person manages to overcome after a deadly struggle, the war will surely extend for a long time.

A long spiritual war exhausts the person and they may get to the verge of despair and want to submit to the thought.

Also a long struggle against a thought may fix it in the unconscious mind.

It may add to the mind images which they would not like to have in their mind lest they would lead afterwards to other thoughts, lusts, dreams and suspicions.

Even though one conquers at last, one's mind becomes defiled through the fight.

That is because the thought becomes able to pour in one's mind conflicts, influences and feelings. It also disheartens the senses and leaves an impression on the heart and the body as well.

The thought affects the body.

For example, the adversary reminds someone of a quarrel between them and someone else; they slacken in dismissing the thoughts and begin to remember the details of the whole quarrel. Their anger is aroused again and their body becomes hot, blood runs into their veins, their eyes get red, and their features become gloomy. Here they begin to think how they will avenge themselves.

Listen to David the prophet describing the stress of thoughts,

"How long, O Lord? Will You forget me forever? How long will You hide Your face from me? How long shall I take counsel in my soul, having sorrow in my heart daily? How long will my enemy be exalted over me? ... Enlighten my eyes, lest I sleep the sleep of death, lest my enemy say, I have prevailed against him." (Ps. 13:1-4).

Flee then from the thought and do not retain it because you do not know where it would lead you or where it would end.

Fleeing away from a thought demonstrates also humility of heart, which is the greatest weapon by which one can defeat the devil.

The person who trusts their own power and ability to fight thoughts, may be forsaken by grace for sometime, so that when they go deep in the war and experiences its violence, they may not boast of their power again. Then they will trust God more than they trust their own will, its steadiness and power. So, God often allows wars to fight people so that one may gain humility.

Nothing vexes the devil more than your refusal to argue with him!!

The first step towards the fall of our mother Eve was the argument with the serpent. Through their talk, the devil was able to direct the mind and senses of Eve and she became a toy in his hands, under his control and influence.

Through argument with an evil thought, you fall within its scope.

At least it feels that you do not object to deal with it. Many sinful relations began with argument and resistance and ended in submission. So, refusing to deal with a thought is an express dismissal from the beginning and letting no chance for it to try to influence you.

You may accept a thought and not know how to bring it out. So refusing it and avoiding any dealing with it is the proper solution.

Retaining a thought may enable it to have dominion and if it continues for a long time one will be a servant to it.

Bondage Of Thought

If the thought dominates a person, it does not only lead them to fall but moreover leads them to continuous submission and bondage to it. When the thought finds that it has reached the heart, and the person wants it, it will knock continuously.

The thought may remain for days or weeks within the mind of the person. Every now and then, it adds something new which settles with it also dismissing every good thought. The person then sleeps with the thought in his mind and awakens with it, walks and works while the thought exists within him. But how can a person conquer?

How To Overcome A Thought

The first method conforms with the saying; 'Prevention is better than a cure'!!!

Don't think that that you can overcome a thought by your own strength because you may win one time and be defeated another. But be internally immune through positive spiritual work which will protect your heart against thoughts.

Arrange for yourself a strong continuous spiritual program which consists of prayers, psalms, spiritual reading, meditations, songs and hymns, spiritual meetings, spiritual company and perpetual spiritual nourishment which would fill the heart with pure feelings. Then the words of our Lord would apply to you;

"A *good man out of the good treasure of his heart brings forth good things..*" while, *"An evil man out of the treasure of his heart brings forth evil things."(Luke 6:45)*

Your heart then is the source of the thoughts. If its feelings are spiritual, it will bring forth spiritual thoughts and if evil thoughts come to it from outside, it will refuse them.

I wish that we would give care to the heart and store in it spiritual matters instead of wasting our spiritual lives in struggling against thoughts.

Be sure that if you always occupy your mind with pure spiritual thoughts, the evil thoughts will find no place within you and you will have no need at all to fight them. Hence we notice that the evil thoughts often trouble a person in the time when they are relaxing or idle. As the mind at that time is void of any spiritual work, the devil comes and settles within it. If however the mind is engaged in prayers, spiritual reading or a spiritual meditation, the thoughts will not prevail in it.

You may ask at this point, 'Do not thoughts fight a person while they are spiritually active? The answer is they fight but do not prevail over you nor trouble you.

Saints were fought by thoughts but were not troubled or defeated by them for they said along with St. Paul, "...*bringing every thought into captivity to the obedience of Christ.*" (2Cor.10:5).

Engaging oneself in spiritual matters dismisses any thoughts, provided that one is deeply occupied with them. Shallow reading or prayers would not dismiss the thoughts. That is why some minds are distracted during prayers.

Live in a state of deep spirituality and by God's grace evil thoughts will not be able to disturb you.

A Question And An Answer

When I remember my sins, I fall in them again, am I still required to do as David the Prophet said, "*My sin is ever before me...*" (Ps.51.:3)?

It is not intended by these words that you remember the offensive details which would trouble you. It is sufficient in this case that you remember your sin in general not in detail.

Also, the holy fathers said that the sins of lust or passions fight the person by causing them to remember.

Suppose that you longed for a certain position or desired to have a thing which you love or fell into a carnal lust, etc the remembrance of the details of those sins may trouble you.

Likewise envy or desire for revenge. The remembrance of the details of these may trouble you. Of such sins we say in the Holy Liturgy, *"The memory of evil that entails death..."*

So, you can remember your sins in humility to repent for them and be humbled but if you find that remembrance would defile your mind or bring lust into your heart or would arouse your anger, envy, desire to avenge or love of the world, then dismiss them immediately. Remembrance of the sin is just the means to a goal for the devil.

Perform any spiritual practice wisely and do not follow 'to the letter' the practice of virtues.

CHAPTER 8

OUTER APPERANCES

Attacked In Both Testaments

The Lord Jesus Christ attacked the love of outer appearances while rebuking the hypocrite scribes and Pharisees. He said, *"Woe to you, scribes and Pharisees, hypocrites! For you cleanse the outside of the cup and dish, but inside they are full of extortion and self-indulgence."* and also, *"Woe to you... For you are like whitewashed tombs which indeed appear beautiful outwardly but inside are full of dead men's bones and all uncleanness." (Matt.23:25,27).*

God's attitude was the same in the Old Testament. God did not accept manifestations such as celebrating the new moons (beginnings of months), fasting, prayers, incense and sacrifices because they practiced them with impure hearts! He says in Isaiah, *"'To what purpose is the multitude of your sacrifices to Me? says the Lord... Bring no more futile sacrifices; incense is an abomination to Me.... Your New Moons and your appointed feasts My soul hates; they are a trouble to Me, I am weary of bearing them. When you spread your hands, I will hide My eyes from you; even though you make many prayers, I will not hear. Your hands are full of blood." (Isa.1:11-15).*

God looks at the heart before anything else, not at outer appearances.

He says, *"Keep your heart with all diligence, for out of it spring the issues of life." (Prov. 4:23)* and also, *"My son give Me your heart, and let your eyes observe My ways." (Prov. 23:26).*

Virtues which do not come from the heart out of love are refused by God. God does not love outer appearances but wants the inner person. He wants the feelings, the emotions and the love of the person not any external act of no value.

A prayer from a pure or humble heart is accepted while the prayer of the wicked is refused.

Therefore, God accepted the prayer of the tax collector and refused that of the Pharisee because it was mingled with pride, boasting and condemning others. God refused also the prayers of those whom He addressed saying *"Your hands are full of blood." (Isa. 1:15).)*

The Holy Bible tells us;

"The sacrifice of the wicked is an abomination to the Lord" (Prov.15:8), "The sacrifice of the wicked is an abomination; how much more when he brings it with wicked intent" (Prov.21:27), and, *"One who turns away his ear from hearing the law, even his prayer shall be an abomination."(Prov.28:9).*

So, we must focus on inner purity which is the real source of every outer purity.

Internal Not External Purity

Sometimes some preachers, ministers and educators concentrate on outer purity alone giving all concern to it. With respect to a girl for example, They look at her appearance, whether her dress is modest or not, whether her make-up is extravagant or not and they concentrate their preaching on such passive matters. They neglect the inner motive lying within the heart that leads the girl to be this way!

Concentration ought to be on one's interior, on the love of God, love of virtue and purity of heart. When the heart becomes pure and gets rid of the motives leading a girl to be extravagant in her appearance, she herself will forsake such appearances.

Rebuke, violence and pressure are not means for refinement. They may change the outer appearance only. But the heart remains unchanged, having the same desires and lusts and perhaps adds to them grumbling, suppression of one's emotions and distress. On the other hand, if the heart is purified, it will carry out any advice with pleasure in a more spiritual way.

Another example is that of a young man who lets his hair grow and wears clothes which do not suit a pious young man. Such a person needs to know what manhood means, what the aspects of a strong personality are, how he can gain the respect of others and besides all this how he can gain purity of the heart. If he is convinced of all this, surely he will get rid of such faults without rebuke or force.

It is not important to cleanse the outside of the cup while the inside is still filthy. Refining the interior is firmer and more stable. Through this a person can truly change and there will be no contradiction between the inside and the outside. If this is the case, the person is not subject to any pressure which may make them seek to escape such outer pressure!

Let us then find out the internal causes which lead to outer wrongdoing so that we may treat them.

For example, take lying. Would a person who lies be reformed through being preached to or by being rebuked? Would it not be more effective for them and for their benefit to discover the reasons that make them lie? Whether it is their fear of something being revealed, or the desire to obtain a certain benefit or whether it is out of boasting or to cover awkwardness or has become a habit without having a reason for that or whether he means by this jesting or vexing others or because he takes pleasure in mocking others!!! We have to find out the reason for lying and treat it and convince a liar that it is of no benefit to lie. We have also to provide them with practical solutions to help them get rid of lying or provide some faultless substitutes. For example, they can keep silent, avoid giving a reply or give a question in answer to a question addressed to them, apologise for a fault instead of covering it with a lie, be convinced that boasting and mocking others are wrong and be convinced also that he can gain people's confidence and respect through being truthful.

In this way we treat the inside and thereupon the outer faults will be removed. So, we should not neglect the outside completely. But how and why?

We Ought Not To Neglect The Outside

Being concerned about the inside does not mean that we can neglect our external actions.

We ought to be examples for others, knowing that our wrong doings may offend. The Lord says in this respect, *"Let your light so shine before men, that they may see your good works and glorify your Father in heaven." (Matt. 5:16).* This verse teaches us that the purpose is to glorify God not ourselves. Also, *"Have regard for good things in the sight of all men." (Rom. 12:17).*

This is how God's children ought to be, as St. John the beloved also says, "...*whoever has been born of God does not sin... In this the children of God...are manifest...*" *(1 Jn. 3:9,10).*

With regard to offences, the Lord says, *"'Woe to that man by whom the offence comes!"* *(Matt. 18:7).*

Then, a person must behave well outwardly provided that:

1- This shall be with the purpose of glorifying God not glorifying oneself.

2- The outer conduct shall be natural due to inner purity of the heart.

If you have not yet attained purity of the heart within, force yourself to do so.

It is true that out of the abundance of the heart the mouth speaks but if your inner feelings are not yet pure with respect to some people, this is not an excuse to sin against them with your tongue so that your tongue and your heart may be the same! Rather be careful with your tongue what you say. Afterwards, you can train your heart to be as good as your tongue.

So, forcing oneself to do good and the desire to gain people's respect and love are required for a person of good outer conduct.

This is not hypocrisy but a kind of self-restraint. Self-restraint outwardly is necessary and required. It is one of the spiritual practices which help a person to attain the life of purity.

Cleanse the interior then, so that it may conform with the proper outer form, but do not fall down to the level of the impure inner man.

You ought to be pure within and without; So try to attain both, and if you begin with one, end with the other also.

To be outwardly on your guard is recommended but do not be satisfied with it alone, add to it inner purity. Let this be your practice with respect to all virtues.

Practices Concerning Virtues

Take fasting as an example with respect to outer behaviour and inner action.

Fasting is not a mere external virtue concerning the body alone in which the body abstains from having the food it desires and abstains completely from having any food for a certain time. When fasting one must also abstain from doing wrong so that restraint of body goes side by side with self -restraint.

If a person has not yet attained such a spiritual level within, they ought not to break his fasting or have any food! Otherwise such a person would fall body and soul! So a person has to train their heart within to adapt itself to the fasting of the body without. Even though this needs struggle, time, and practice, it will be achieved through God's grace.

Here, we may lay down a spiritual rule which would set a balance between the internal and the external level. **The rule is:**

If either the internal or the external is high while the other is low, raise the low level to the high one.

Never be satisfied with outer proper conduct because God looks at the heart. Struggle always to purify your heart and to make your outer good conduct a mere preparation or training to attain the good inner action.

Often, outer purity is a means for inner purity!! For example, a young person fights with inner carnal lusts and impure feelings which do not conform with chastity and which perhaps bring them unclean dreams. Would such a person behave in the same way outwardly so that his interior would conform with his outer conduct? Of course not. For in this way they would destroy themselves and add to the sins of the mind and the heart, sins of action, senses and body!

Such a person must be on their guard externally and this would help them to attain inner purity. They must not be satisfied with being on their guard externally.

Therefore, do not get desperate and say, 'What is the use of outer purity if I am not clean within! What is the use of chastity of the body if my soul is an adulterer!'

This is a war of the devil to make you fall into despair and in sin.

Your outer resistance means that you refuse sin. Add to it resistance against thoughts and be sure that God will send you His grace to help you. Because of your external honesty, God will help you within as long as you resort to Him and ask His help.

Be faithful in what is least - i.e. The outside - and God will grant you in abundance, i.e., inner purity. At the same time, do not neglect your interior because God wants the heart. Struggle within also.

Enter the battle against internal thoughts and as you conquered in the battle of the body and the senses, you will conquer here also. Both matters will co-operate. Your awareness without will protect you. from many internal wars, or at least you will not be fought in two fields at the same time. Your outside awareness will make you on your guard in your whole life and will help you experience internal awareness also. To all this will be added the grace from on-high which God will send you as a reward for your faithfulness.

Beginners may be satisfied with victory in outer wars but afterwards they proceed into inner wars which are much harder and deeper but lead to the purity of the heart and the mind. Thus, the heart becomes a temple for God.

Purity of the heart means that it refuses sin and hates it. Once attained it helps to fully conquer in outer wars, as such wars no longer will have power over it. Hence if sin comes to a person in a dream while they are not aware, their unconscious mind will be fully on guard and refuse it. So they will not sin even in their dream because their heart and mind refuse sin. If sin presses hard on them in a dream to commit it, they will wake up because their heart refuses to sin, as the Apostle says, "...*he cannot sin...* " (*1Jn. 3:9).*

The Apostle mentions the reasons for this saying, *"... for His seed remains in him,..."* He says also, *"...he keeps himself and the wicked one does not touch him,..."* (1 *Jn. 5:18).*

This is the passive side concerning sin. what about the positive side?

When the heart becomes pure, all its virtuous acts will have a spiritual motive and will be done for God's sake only.

For God's Sake Not For People's Sake

One must not do good in order to be exalted in one's own eyes or in the eyes of others for both matters are included in the sin of vain glory and leads to hypocrisy. The speech of the Lord Jesus Christ about the scribes and Pharisees is obvious; *"But all their works they do to be seen by men." (Matt.23:5).*

Thus they fall in the sin of the love of outer appearances. Whatever good they do is false because it is mingled with self-love and vain glory; so its aim is not pure. Its aim is not God's love or the love of good for itself and is not due to a pure nature. Here some may ask, 'Does this mean that we must not do good before people at all so that they may not see us or praise us for it!!' Of course not, for the Holy Bible says, *"Have regards for good things in the sight of all men." (Rome.12:17).*

With regard to praise, the Apostles and holy people were praised by people, even after their departure and it was not a sin. It is unreasonable that a righteous person abstains from doing good completely to avoid people's praise!!

Where then is the wisdom to fulfill the commandment of doing good in secret. The Lord says, *"But you, when you pray, go into your room, and when you have shut your door, pray to your Father who is in the secret place, and your father who sees in secret will reward you openly." (Matt. 6:6),* and *"When you do a charitable deed do not let your left hand know what your right hand is doing." (Matt. 6:3),* and also, *"...so that you do not appear to men to be fasting, but to your Father who is in the secret place..." (Matt. 6:18).*

From all this we conclude:

+ Do good in secret as much as you can.

Many times, you may not be able because you go to church in the sight of people and pray, attend meetings regularly, partake continuously of Holy Communion, fast all the fasts of the church and your ministry is perhaps known in the church. Your charity to the poor may be known such as in the case of Anba Abram the Bishop of Fayoum, Ibrahim El Gohari and Anba Sarabamoan Abu Tarha (the veiled) What can you do in this case?

+ It is not a sin if people know the good deeds you do but the sin is to make the aim of doing good to let people see and praise you!!

This is what the Lord Jesus Christ meant when He said, *"Therefore, when you do a charitable deed, do not sound a trumpet before you as the hypocrites do in the synagogues and in the streets, that they may have glory from men." (Matt.6:2)* The Lord said also, *"For they love to pray standing in the synagogues, and on the corners of the streets, that they may be seen by men." (Matt. 6:5)* and also *"...for they disfigure their faces that they may appear to men to be fasting..." (Matt.6:16).*

It is obvious here that the aim is to be seen by people and to be praised by them. This is ostentatious or love of outer appearances.

So, if you do good out of a heart void of any ostentation and not have the aim of being seen by people but rather prefer to avoid this, do not worry if people know what good you do.

+ Avoid being seen by people but if they know, do not let that affect your heart. Forget that and give no heed to it.

St. Paul the Apostle says about his ministry and that of his assistants *"By honour and dishonor, by evil report and good report..." (2 Cor. 6:8)*. His heart did not boast either with honour or with good report.

St. Macarius the Great taught to be as a dead person who gives no heed to honour or dishonor.

+ If praise reaches your ears and is heard by you, do not allow it to enter your heart but remember your weakness and your sins to overcome it.

+ Even with regard to the public deeds, you can conceal certain things. For example, people may know that you are fasting but you can conceal the level of this fasting whether with respect to the time of abstinence or the kind of food you eat. If some know this do not let all the others know it as well.

The same can be said with respect to charity. They may know that you are charitable, but not the amount that you give.

Some may know that you pray but do not know the condition of your heart during prayers.

Some may know this in the case of public prayers such as the prayers of the priests in the holy liturgies. In this regard I advise the priest to forget completely that there are people listening to him and to concentrate only on that he is standing in the presence of God addressing Him alone whether people hear him on not.

If a priest puts in his mind to please people with his prayers, he falls into vain glory! In such a case, the prayer is not addressed to God, but to people and for the sake of oneself!

The same can be said in the case of a priest who performs many activities for the sole purpose of pleasing people, not to serve the kingdom of heaven. Such a priest falls into vain glory. The matter becomes worse if such works are mere activities and projects without any spirituality.

CHAPTER 9

SINS OF THE TONGUE

Dangers Of The Tongue

The tongue is a two-edged sword which can be used in doing good or in doing evil. So the Holy Bible says, *"For by your words you will be justified, and by your words will be condemned." (Matt.12:37).*

The Lord said to the wicked servant, *"Out of your own mouth I will judge you, you wicked servant..." (Luke 19:22).* David the Prophet also said to the young man who informed him of the death of Saul the King, *"...your own mouth has testified against you." (2 Sam.1:16)* and when St. Peter spoke, the people said to him, *"...your speech betrays you." (Matt 26:73).*

The Lord tells us about the danger of idle words, *"But I say to you that for every idle word men may speak, they will give account of it in the day of judgment." (Matt.12:36).*

An idle word does not only mean an evil word but also a word which is of no benefit.

God did not create the tongue for nothing but for a certain use which it ought to perform else it would be idle. It is not the task of the tongue to err but it has a positive role. For is it reasonable that a certain machine has no use but to do no harm to anyone!! Or does it have to do some useful work! The same is the case of the tongue. So, idle talk is one of the sins of the tongue:

Idle talk is to make wrong use of the tongue, which may also be in an annoying way. It also wastes the time of the hearer as well as the time of the speaker.

The tongue may be useful or harmful, as the Apostle exclaims saying, *"Does a spring send forth fresh water and bitter from the same opening..."(James. 3:11).*

St. James the Apostle explains in detail the danger of the tongue. He says, *"If anyone does not stumble in word, he is a perfect man, able also to bridle the whole body... " (James 3:2).*

He says also, *"Even so the tongue is a little member and boasts great things. see how great a forest a little fire kindles! And the tongue is a fire, a world of iniquity...it defiles the whole body and sets on fire the course of nature; and it is set on fire by hell." (James 3:5,6).*

The tongue is so dangerous that its sin is considered filth and uncleanness. The Lord Jesus Christ says, *"Not what goes into the mouth defiles a man; but what comes out of the mouth, this defiles a man." (Matt.15:11).*

So, uncleanness is not only sins of fornication for example but also sins of the tongue! This demonstrates how dangerous the sins of the tongue are.

Faults Of The Tongue

Many and uncounted are the faults and the sins in which the tongue falls, among which are:

Sins due to pride.

They include boasting, self-justification, obstinacy, arguing and interrupting others while talking so that one may lead the talk arrogantly.

Sins of lying.

Examples· of such sins are; explicit lies, exaggeration, half-truths, delusion, deceit, misleading, trumping up, false testimony, equivocation and beguiling.

Sins contradicting love.

Such as insults, rage, reviling and loathing, condemning others, derogatory comments, scorning people, defaming them, slander, calumny, intrigues and also threatening words, taunting, disclosing others' secrets, evading responsibility and putting it on the shoulders of the others and spreading rumours.

Sins due to cruelty.

Such as hurting, painful words which do not mind the feelings of others and also threatening and frightening words etc.

Unchaste words.

Such words may be uttered through filthy stories, impudent fun, shameless songs, sexual and tempting words, shameless words, impolite and insolent conduct and whatever a good and pure ear feels ashamed to hear.

Sins of the tongue concerning belief.

Examples of this are words of blasphemy, spreading suspicions concerning religion and dogma, spreading heresies and heterodoxies and misleading the believers with them, using

God's name in vain and perverting the minds with superstitions.

Sins which show a base soul.

Such as words of flattery, false praise, approving of the mistakes of others, double talk, adhering to peer pressure, hypocrisy, flattery, complaining and grumbling, words expressing fear and despair.

An Important Remark

There are others which resemble the sins of the tongue though not exactly the same. We mean by such sins the words not uttered but written or printed. These are the same type of sins and the same war but perhaps, more awful than the sins of the tongue are because a person who writes down or prints such words is unaware of being responsible for such words.

Anyhow, the sin is the same. It is the same whether you insult someone by word of, mouth or by writing. The insult is the same as it makes light of the person and their feelings. The psychological motives are also the same. Only the responsibility of this act differs in that the insult is not uttered but written.

Perhaps the reason is that it is easier to address someone in writing than face to face! Usually, a person dares to write words which they cannot utter face to face!

Anyhow the sins of the tongue reveal other sins which go side by side with them and even lead to them. Those are the sins originating from the heart.

Sins Originating From The Heart

A person may be enraged, and in his anger may utter harsh and improper words, yet their friends sometimes make excuses for them saying that in spite of his faults his heart is pure. This is obviously wrong because a pure heart utters pure words as the Holy Bible says, *"For out of the abundance of the heart the mouth speaks." (Matt./2:34)* and also, *"A good man out of the good treasure of his heart brings forth good things, and an evil man out of the evil treasure brings forth evil things....for a tree is known by its fruit." (Matt.12:35,33).*

So, sinful words show a sinful heart and thus the sin of the tongue here is a double sin.

Harsh words show a cruel heart and arrogant words show a proud heart. Likewise rash words show a reckless heart and spiteful words show a malevolent heart and so on. Therefore, whoever wants to improve their speech, must first reform their heart. Otherwise such a person will be insincere uttering words which contradict the feelings of their heart or tries to show inner feelings which do not conform with what they says

So, the sins of the tongue are not merely sins of the tongue but they are in fact compound sins.

The sin of the tongue usually come in the second or third stage!!

A Second Or Aa Third Sin

Take for example the sin of lying.

Seldom lying is the first sin but it is often, or always born of a 'mother' sin. A person lies to conceal another sin and lying is often accompanied by a third sin, which is fear. Then there is a sin which one wants to conceal, accompanied by fear - which is considered a second sin -and both result in lying, as a third sin. Often, a person confesses to the priest that they lied but do not mention the other two sins...

Outrage also is a third or a fourth sin. Harsh or cruel words uttered in outrage are not out of nothing but they originate from other sins, such as self-love, concern about dignity or benefit, intolerance, cruelty and disliking someone or not respecting them. These four sins bring forth the sin of uttering harsh words or outrage which is the fifth stage.

Whoever wants to cure themselves of anger and of uttering cruel words, must clean their heart first from· the previous four sins. If a person instead wants to justify themselves by making excuses for their outrage and anger, these same excuses will form a sixth sin which is self-justification.

A spiritual person ought to condemn themselves, not justify themselves!!

The same can be said of any other sins of the tongue, for all of them are compound sins, if analysed, each revealing various sins included in it.

We can add to this point a new element which is control.

Results Out Of One's Control

1. The first result is that the words uttered by you cannot be withdrawn.

You may repent for uttering the words or justify yourself or apologize for saying them but the thing which is out of your control is that someone has heard it and that there are consequent effects.

So the sins of the tongue differ from those of the mind or the heart because the latter are within you, affecting you alone and are not revealed to others.

2. The second result is the effect of the sins of the tongue on those to whom they are addressed:

Suppose you bear a grudge against someone and have strong feelings of ill will against them, the matter is still within your heart. This does not make the relation between you and them bad or worse. But if you reveal your feelings through offensive words, how will you make up for this? The matter is no longer a sin within you but it developed into an external relation. You may try to fix the relation but you fail, or you try to reconcile with the person whom you offended but they refuse. The reaction to your words still dominates over their heart and they may not be able to forgive easily.

Suppose your offensive words were heard by others, the scope of the offence will be much wider. The others may feel strongly for him and their feelings towards you may change and they may retaliate. The person whom you offended may forgive you but the others who heard your offensive words may not forgive.

Even the person who is offended and who forgives despite this, may form within him an idea about you which will not be wiped away easily. Likewise, as far as your words hurt, their effect will be deeper. The effect will even increase if your tone and your looks are cruel like your words. This makes the case more complicated. Therefore, whenever you speak, put before you that whatever you say will not be forgotten.

You can give vent to your inner feelings but it is a thing to be regretted that you forget the feelings and sensations of the person who listens to you. You do not think how this might affect them or what others may think when they hear you talking in such a way or hear indirectly what you have said.

Thus the words of the Holy Bible prove true, *"By your words you will be condemned..." (Matt.12:37).*

3. The third result is that you may repent for such sins but the person who hears you may not repent and God would require his blood from you. Your words may raise a certain sin in the mind or the heart of that person. It may be the sin of doubt in case your words raise doubts. Their heart may change towards some people whom you spoke ill against because they believed what you said falsely. This may affect them and they may repeat the shameless stories and foul jokes which you told and thus they and those who hear them repeating them will be affected. Then you repent but the person who heard them does not repent. What would you do?

How can you treat the sins of such a person who sinned because of your words? Or would you like that their sins are counted against you and you be condemned for them even, even though you repented!

There may be certain sins of the tongue which you do not know and you will be condemned for them because you are not aware of their extent.

How easy it is for you to provide people with a wrong principle to follow. You may correct it within you while the others take it as a rule for their lives.

In fact, the sins of the tongue are not barren, for they bring forth many others.

In order to know how serious the sins of the tongue are, let us hearken to the words of the Lord in the Sermon on the Mount where he says, "...*whoever says to his brother, "Raca!" shall be in danger of the council. But whoever says, "You fool!" shall be in danger of hell fire."* (Matt.5:22).

St. Augustine explains that the word 'Raca' is the least word which expresses lack of respect. So, one must be fully on guard against the sins of the tongue, cruel words and words of sarcasm and mockery.

Caution When Speaking

The first rule is to be slow to speak.

Do not be hasty to speak, especially when you are anxious or angry because you may not be able to control yourself or properly choose your words. Here, I remind you of the words of St. James the Apostle, *"...let every man be swift to hear, slow to speak, slow to wrath; for the wrath of man does not produce the righteousness of God." (James 1:19,20).*

I advise you when you are angry, not to give a quick answer, do not speak nor utter a lie. Calm down first because it is your emotions which will give the answer not your mind nor your soul. So your anger is dangerous for you and for anyone that listens to you and you may not be able to correct the results.

If you are a leader or a clergyman or a father, do not give yourself the right to speak without restraint or without minding the feelings of others.

The elders or those who are in positions of authority often give themselves more rights than they ought to have. Often they do not respect the feelings of others who are younger or subordinates, taking as an excuse that they have to rebuke, correct and teach. I remind these people of the words of the Apostle, *"Let all things be done decently and in. order." (1Cor.14:40)* and *"Let all that you do be done with love." (1 Cor. 16:14).* I remind them also of the fruit of the Spirit, *"...Kindness..." (Gal. 5:22).*

It is a thing to be regretted that those who have authority over others would lose their eternity just for rebuking those who are younger than they! It is also regrettable that they think that because they have authority, they do not need to follow the rules. They think that God will no longer require them to be meek, humble, tender and decent. It is as if they have become above the commandments.

So, do not think highly of yourself but be always careful in your talk.

Many holy persons found that silence is a useful remedy for the sins of the tongue. The Psalmist says in this respect "...*set a guard, O Lord, over my mouth; Keep watch over the door of my lips.*" *(Ps.141:3);* and St. Arsenius, the teacher of the sons of the kings has this famous saying, *'Many a time have I talked and repented; but for silence, I never repented'.*

Try then to train yourself to be silent and if you do speak let it be out of necessity. When you do speak be brief and relevant, in a calm sedate voice. Remember that it is said of the Lord Jesus Christ, "*...He will not quarrel nor cry out, nor will anyone hear His voice in the streets.*" *(Matt.12:19).*

Do not be eager to teach others or to speak about your knowledge and experience. Be aware that any mistake - particularly in the field of religion - has more serious consequences than just offending the feelings of others. St. James warns us in this concern saying, "*My brethren, let not many of you become teachers knowing that we shall receive a stricter judgment. For we all stumble in many things.*" *(James 3:1,2).*

I advise you further to always talk to others decently with good manners. I may return to this point in another book entitled. 'Silence and Talking' if God wills.

Try to take a lesson from all your previous faults of the tongue. Let every word you utter be measured by accurate scales. Let your words be of benefit.

CHAPTER 10

CRUELTY OF THE HEART

Two types of cruelty.

Cruelty of the heart is in two forms: cruelty towards God and cruelty towards people.

• Cruelty towards God is the continuous refusal of God and closing the heart before Him. In this case, we are not affected by God's kindness and the love He shows towards us nor by His knocking at the doors of our hearts.

• Cruelty towards people happens when one is harsh in action, uses cruel words, severe looks and uses cruel punishment and severe reproach. It may also be physical/bodily cruelty by tormenting someone or towards their soul by humiliating, destroying or defaming them.

A sinner falls in both types of cruelty.

The opposite of cruelty is; mercy, kindness, tenderness and compassion. The Lord Jesus Christ talked much about mercy. He said, *"Blessed are the merciful, for they shall obtain mercy." (Matt.5.:7).* He even made mercy a condition for inheriting the Kingdom of heaven (Matt. 25:35,36). He told us how the rich man was deprived of the kingdom of heaven because he did not show compassion towards Lazarus (Luke 16:21).

The Attitude Of The Lord Jesus Christ Towards Cruelty

The Lord Jesus Christ was compassionate to the adulterers and sinners. He used to accept the repentant who came to Him in tears and treated them kindly, as He did when He defended the woman who was a sinner and was taken in adultery, in the very act (Jn. 8:7).

But at the same time, He did not accept the cruel people at all but rebuked them severely. He rebuked the Scribes and Pharisees who were severe in teaching religion; *"...For they bind heavy burdens, hard to hear, and lay them on men's shoulders; but they themselves will not move them with one of their fingers..." (Matt.23:4))*.

So, the Lord addressed them saying, *"But woe to you, scribes and Pharisees, hypocrites! For you shut up the Kingdom of heaven against men; for you neither go in yourselves, nor do you allow those who are entering to go in." (Matt.23:13)*.

Cruelty is often an aspect or a result of pride. Therefore, the Lord is against the proud, as the Holy Bible says, *"God resists the proud..." (1Pet. 5:5, James4:6)*.

Thus, God calls us always to be kind-hearted and tender and at the same time He warns the cruel that they will be treated in the same manner they treat others. He says, *"For with what judgment you judge, you will be judged; and with the same measure you use, it will be measured back to you." (Matt. 7:1,2)*.

Let them who are cruel then, beware and fear the result of their own cruelty upon themselves.

Cruelty is a diabolic war, and whoever is cruel resembles the devil in his attributes. For cruelty is not an attribute of God who is always merciful and compassionate upon all.

Cruelty is not hated by God alone but also by the righteous who have tender hearts. We see Jacob the Patriarch rebuking his two sons Simeon and Levi for their cruelty. He says, *"Cursed be their. anger, for it is fierce; and their wrath, for it is cruel."* *(Gen.49:7)*.

A kind heart is near to God, it is like a soft dough in the hand of God which He can form as He wills. The wicked on the other hand have, cruel hearts, as hard as stone, that do not submit to the work of God within them. St. Paul warns us against such cruelty saying, *"Today, if you will hear His voice, do not harden your hearts..." (Heb. 3:15,8,4:7)*.

God always considers sin as hard-heartedness because a sensitive heart never disobeys God or closes its doors before Him. It is sensitive to God's voice and call and it responds quickly to Him. A sensitive heart is easily affected by God's dealings and the acts of His grace. Even if this heart goes astray, it will quickly yearn for returning. The smallest event may affect such a heart and every word of God makes it soften and return to Him. Unlike this was Pharaoh's cruel heart. He did not yield or repent at all however severe the blows were!

So, the repentance of a cruel heart is not easy and its sensitivity to the means of grace is very weak, temporary and transient. It may not even be affected at all!

This brings us to an important point.

The Attributes Of The Cruel Heart

A cruel heart is not mindful in its dealing with God. The word of God does not affect this heart. An example of this is the people of Sodom whom Lot told about God's wrath and warned them but *"...he seemed as one that mocked unto his sons in law..."* *(Gen. 19:14).* The word of God to such cruel people is like the seeds which fall on stone.

A hard-hearted person not only is not affected by the words of the Spirit but also may mock and laugh at them and may even refuse to listen!

If a person has a heart that is cruel towards God, they will avoid any place where the word of God may be spoken. They will refuse to go to church or to any meetings. They neglect the Holy Bible and the prayers and any spiritual practices, for they no longer affect them. God's commandments become heavy for them but in fact the load is within their heart. Their heart is too cruel to be affected by any spiritual motive. Nothing affects them whether it be God's kindness, warnings or punishment, or any accidents or events. No illness nor departure of their beloved, no prayers nor spiritual words affect them. Even God's loving kindnesses are received by them with ingratitude, or they attribute them to human causes. To such a person applies the words of the Lord, *"All day long I have stretched out My hands to a disobedient and contrary people." (Rom. 10:21).*

Thus, cruelty of the heart leads to disobedience and resistance.

You may continue for long hours explaining to a person who did something wrong, what their fault is but they will insist on their attitude as if you had said nothing. They also refuse to confess their fault because theirs is the stony heart which does not respond.

What a tragedy it would be if grace forsakes such a person, for the Lord says, *"So I gave them over to their own stubborn heart, to walk in their own counsels."(Ps.81.·12)* and also, *"God gave them to a debased mind, to do things which are not fitting...", "For this reason God gave them up to vile passions..."* *(Rom.1:28,26).*

So if cruelty of the heart continues it becomes very dangerous to the salvation of a person because it makes God forsake a person and the person is destroyed.

The tears of a sensitive person flow easily but the eyes of a cruel person seldom shed tears whatever the reasons may be. This is because tears reveal tender feelings but a cruel person is not tender in his dealings with God or with people. On the contrary, their hard-heartedness leads them to fury and anger.

A cruel person is quickly inflamed with rage against others, becomes furious and excited, makes threats and cannot endure a word against them. Yet, at the same time, they give no heed to the feelings of others; they hurt them easily and rashly. They readily insult others and confront them and do not mind how their words would affect others. Here a cruel person combines two contradictory behaviors. They are very sensitive concerning how people treat them but are not at all sensitive concerning the effect of their own manners on others.

When such a person rebukes someone, their reproach is excessive and when they get angry, their anger lasts long and is violent. In their cruelty, they do not bear with anyone, yet they want all others to bear with them and not be offended by their rage but rather consider it their due!

So cruelty causes aversion and whoever yields to it, loses people and fail in their social life. So all of us must be on our guard against the cruelty of the heart, as the Apostle advises us, "...*be kind to one another...*" *(Eph. 4:32).* Remember also the fruits of the Spirit; gentleness, kindness and longsuffering and also love and peace. (Gal. 5:22,23).

Hence it is important to know the causes of cruelty of the heart so as to avoid them.

The Causes Of Cruelty Of The Heart.

As for cruelty towards God, the main reason is love of sin.

Love of sin.

Love of sin captivates the heart and makes a person attached to sin. They forget God and everything related to Him and even considers God as an enemy who wants to deprive them of the sin which they love. This hardens their heart towards God.

Perhaps for this reason, the Holy Bible says, "*...friendship with the world is enmity with God.*" *(James 4:4).*

Also, the rich youth, for the love of money, was hard hearted against the Lord Jesus Christ and left Him and went away sorrowful (Matt. 19:22). Also Lot's wife, who loved the goods of Sodom, was hard hearted. Even when the angel was holding her hand to get her away, she did not see God who saved her nor His love but looked back at Sodom and became a pillar of salt (Gen.

19:26).

A more obvious example is Pharaoh whose heart was hardened because he loved authority and loved to benefit from the service of a whole people. So, he did not benefit from all the miracles and the blows which took place.

Another example is the atheist/existentialists who liked to enjoy being away from God's commandments due to their love for the world. These are so hard hearted that they even denied the existence of God. Their philosopher said, 'It is better for me that God does not exist so that I may exist.'!

The love of sin had its effect on Samson the Judge of Israel. It made him forget his vow and his dignity and reveal the secret of his power. He forgot everything because at that very moment his heart was hardened against God.

Let us not forget that cruelty of the heart makes a person hold fast to sin and postpone repentance. Whenever this person hears the voice of God within their heart, they find the voice of sin and love of the world and fleshly desires prevailing. So their heart hardens and refuses the act of grace.

Evil company

A heart may be hardened because of evil company and its bad effect on the person.

Take for example Ahab the King and see how his wicked wife Jezebel made his heart harden. Ahab was distressed because he wanted to take the vineyard of Naboth the Jezreelite; *"...and he lay down on his bed, and turned away his face, and would eat no food." (1 Kings 21:4).* But Jezebel made a plan by which Naboth was to be accused of blasphemy against God and the king and thus be killed and his vineyard go to Ahab. Thereupon, Ahab's heart was hardened and he got up forgetting his distress and despair and carried out the plan and Naboth was killed.

Another example of the bad influence of evil company is the case of Rehoboam the Son of Solomon who followed the advice of the young men concerning dealing with the people who requested of him to make the yoke upon them lighter. The elders advised Rehoboam to speak good words to the congregation of Israel gently and lovingly. They said to him, *"If you will be a servant to these people today, and serve them, and answer them, and speak good words to them, then they will be your servants forever." (1 Kings 12:7).* But the young men hardened his heart and convinced him of the importance of authority and dignity and that people must· submit to him. The young men said to Rehoboam to address them by saying, *"My little finger will be thicker than my father's waist. And now, whereas my father laid a heavy yoke on you, I will add to your yoke; my father chastised you with whips, but I will chastise you with scourges!" (1Kings 12:10,11).*

Rehoboam behaved according to the counsel of the young men using all his authority and the kingdom was torn out of his hand.

How easy it is for the heart of a youth to be hardened by their evil friends who introduce to them new concepts of power and heroism, of freedom and of the rights they ought to claim. This makes such a youth revolt against any authority or leadership whether at home, school or in the street. They may even revolt against order and against law and consider it maturity to impose their own views.

Many youths in some western countries refuse to submit to their parents when they grow up under the pretext of keeping their personal freedom. A youth takes the advice of their father as a mere opinion which may be right or wrong and which they may follow or not! Hence, their heart hardens against their father and against any spiritual father or guide. They hold to their opinions and insist on their advice even though they are young and of little experience!

We need to bring up our children from their early childhood in such a way that no strange ideas would trap them, spoil them or harden their hearts.

We need to strengthen our children before their hearts are hardened with ideas that would make them argue concerning intuitive matters and refuse anything just for the sake of rebellion. Such ideas may depict to them that obedience is weakness, submission is yielding and calmness is fear and cowardice. Such ideas may turn for them all the scales and they will feel happy because they find in this, self-assertion and a firm personality.

Speaking about the effect of evil company on the heart, we do not mean only persons but we mean also books, printed material, mass media and audiovisual media. So we must insure that such things are not evil influences.

What is said concerning the young, may apply also to the grown-ups. Let us take the family as an example.

A step mother may harden the heart of her husband against his children from a previous wife. She keeps talking to him about their faults and how serious such faults are until he is incited against them and treats them cruelly. Or the mother who fills the ears of her married son with the faults of his wife or the insults which the wife hurts her with till the husband becomes cruel and changes his treatment to his wife.

So, everyone must be cautious and not permit any cruelty to creep towards them from others or believe whatever is said to them.

Pride.

Pride is one of the causes of hard-heartedness. It leads a person to conceit regarding their own dignity and esteem and the people's respect for them. This makes them cruel towards anyone who seems to hurt their dignity in any way.

Cruelty caused by pride appears in one's features and looks, in one's harsh voice, in one's words and style of dealing with others.

Temperament and heredity

Inherited temperament may be among the causes of cruelty but here, there is a question; 'Is a person guilty who inherits a cruel temperament while another is born meek by nature and needs no effort to struggle against an inner cruelty?'

The answer is that a temperament may be changed even though it is inherited and they that exerts themselves to change his temperament shall have a greater reward from God.

We have, in this regard, the example of St. Moses the Black whose temperament changed from being evil and cruel to the opposite. He became meek and loved and served all others. This is only an example but there are other causes for cruelty which have no place here. Now we shall conclude this chapter with a few words about.

The Remedy For Cruelty

Cruelty may be cured through a life of repentance as in the case of St. Moses the Black. This may be achieved by keeping company with the meek and merciful who have a good influence on the person and can be taken as examples. The stories of holy persons known for their meekness, kindness and compassion for everybody is of benefit in this case.

A person can also learn a lesson from the harm incurred every time he was heart-hardened.

Other things which may help to soften the heart are:
- To be aware of the sufferings of society.
- By ministering to the needy, the poor, the ill, the weak, the disabled, the orphans and the widows.
- One can also take art in solving the problems of the others.
- Calm music which may also cure tense nerves.

All this must be accompanied by prayers asking God to change the cruel nature.

CHAPTER 11

SPIRIITUAL LUKEWARMNESS

Fervency And Lukewarmness.

Lukewarmness is the lack of spiritual fervor. The Holy Bible requires us to be *"...fervent in spirit..." (Rom. 12:11)*.

The Holy Spirit descended on the day of Pentecost in the form of tongues of fire (Acts 2:3) on the holy Apostles, inflaming them. God appeared also to Moses the Prophet in a flame of fire out of the midst of a bush (Ex.3:2). And it is said, *"Our God is a consuming fire." (Heb. 12:29)*.

So, any person who has the Spirit of God dwelling in them must be fervent in spirit.

Fervor is in the heart of such a person and it appears in the love they show, in their prayers, in their worship and in their ministry. It is a fervor which encompasses all their life. Wherever they settle, the place becomes inflamed with their fervor, their activity and with the holy zeal in them.

A spiritual person loves God and loves people and the Holy Bible compares love to fire as it is said, *"Many waters cannot quench love." (Song 8:7)*. Hence, a minister who is full of love, burns as if with fire as St. Paul the Apostle said, *"Who is made to stumble, and I do not burn." (2 Cor. 11:29)* The fervor of a spiritual person is transferred to others.

It is also said of the holy angles who do God's work with all fervor and activity; *"Who makes His angels spirits, His ministers a flame of fire." (Ps. 104:4)*.

However, many of God's children who are spiritual do not maintain their fervor but become lukewarm and lose their first love. No doubt there are reasons which lead to this.

They pray but not with the same love, nor with the same depth or spirit. They read the Holy Bible but are not influenced by it. Spiritual meetings and liturgies no longer have any influence on their hearts as before. Their worship becomes like a body without a spirit, *"...having a form of godliness but denying its power." (2Tim. 3:5).* They talk to God but do not feel His existence nor His presence in their lives.

The book of Revelation shows how God hates lukewarmness; He addresses the angel of the church of the Laodiceans saying, *"So then, because you are lukewarm, and neither cold nor hot, I will spew you out of My mouth."* and *"I could wish you were cold or hot..." (Rev. 3:16,15).*

However, lukewarmness is a comparative state, measured according to the condition of the person fought with it. That means what is considered as lukewarm concerning great saints, may be considered as fervor in the case of ordinary persons! In the case of the great saints, languor makes them fall a little from their high levels but they are still much higher than others.

Kinds Of Lukewarmness

There is an ordinary kind of lukewarmness which befalls all people even the saints. There is also a dangerous kind which threatens the spiritual life. A third kind is relative lukewarmness, which appears when we compare different periods in the life of a spiritual person though they are strong in each of them.

+ The ordinary lukewarmness is an aspect of our nature which tends to deviate from a straight path that positively moves forward.

+ As for the dangerous lukewarmness, it continues for a long time and is deep within oneself, without any internal reproach. A person may get used to it and exerts no effort to get out of it. Such a kind of lukewarmness may be a fox in sheep's clothing.

An example of this is a person who becomes so used to the church that they enter it without any veneration, awe, or respect and are no longer affected by being there. They may cause problems, raise their voice and cry out in the church. They may rebuke and behave harshly under the pretext of keeping order; they may interrupt the priest or the deacon while praying in order to correct a linguistic mistake. Such a person may search for their spirituality but find none or perhaps they do not search at all thinking they are doing right.

At this stage, such a person is said to have fallen from lukewarmness to sin without being aware. Also they could be aware but they justify themselves.

Lukewarmness makes a person lose their meekness, humility and their awe for the place they are found in and their respect for others.

Dangerous Signs Of Lukewarmness

Lukewarmness is a falling process... How?

It is falling from love to routine, from spirit to rationalism, from spiritual virtues to virtues of the body or from being concerned only with God to being concerned. with people.

Lukewarmness may be said to be a pause in time, or an outer relation with God without going deep in dealing with Him. It may also have an affect on ones virtues with regard to their quantity, not their quality or depth.

Each of these points needs a long talk but I shall state every point briefly and explain the aspects as well as the causes of lukewarmness.

Falling From Love To Routine

A spiritual life must be all love for God and such love must encompass all virtues. You pray because you love God and you say to Him, *"My soul thirst for You., my flesh longs for You in a dry and thirsty land where there is no water." (Ps. 63:1)* and *"Oh how I love Your law! It is my meditation all the day." (Ps. 119:97).*

But in the case of lukewarmness, prayers may turn into a mere duty or an obligation which you do so that your conscience may not trouble or accuse you of negligence. You may pray unwillingly and so there will be no emotion or fervor in your prayer and it may be without understanding, lacking in spirituality. It will be without humility, solemnity, faith, meditation or love. Suffice to say that your prayer is just routine.

What is said about prayer in the case of lukewarmness may apply to the other spiritual practices.

While in lukewarmness, you read the Holy Bible as a mere routine, without understanding, meditation or applying it to your life. When you read it you are not really interested in the words of God. Unlike this was David the prophet who said, *"I rejoice at Your word as one who finds great treasure" (Ps. 119:162).*

Perhaps you started your spiritual life with love for God but you did not continue in love. Why?

Perhaps this lukewarmness is due to your being concerned about the quantity not the quality and this led you to a formal worship. You want to pray a certain number of psalms and prayers; you want to read a certain number of the Bible chapters and perform a certain number of metania (prostrations). You do all this but are not concerned about how you do them.

Your only concern now is for the quantity not the spirit. If you achieve a certain number of the said practices you will be content and not care whether God is pleased with your manner of worship or not.

St. Isaac advises in this matter, to say to yourself 'I do not stand before God to count words'.

St. Paul the Apostle also prefers speaking five words with understanding than ten thousand words in a tongue (1Cor. 14:19).

Perhaps because you want to perform this duty, you pray in haste and thus you pray without understanding or meditation. Prayer has become an obligation in which your main purpose is to fulfill it!! This obligation is called by the monks a canon (or a law). This law has become your aim instead of enjoying talking with

God in love.

The deviation of the aim from its spiritual course certainly leads you to lukewarmness because it drives you away from the spirituality of prayers that give you fervor.

Many people did not learn the hymns nor the midnight psalmody by heart at the beginning but they used to pray them slowly, so they were able to contemplate on them and pray them with spirit. Through practice they were able to learn them by heart and gradually they came to sing the psalmody so quickly that the words sung were unintelligible, a stranger would not understand what was said! So haste in reciting led to a lack of understanding, feelings and meditation. So, hymns became mere music, void of the spirit of prayer.

If you are fought with any or all of these things say to yourself. 'I want to pray, to speak to God from my heart, even if it just a few words like those of the tax-collector or of the thief on the cross.'

So, one of the causes of lukewarmness may be your being satisfied with reciting -not praying- well learnt prayers without adding to them other prayers from your heart or your feelings.

How deep the psalms and the other learnt prayers are! I wish that you would pray them with understanding with all your heart. They are spiritual treasures! However with the Psalms you need to have your own prayers which you pray with your own words, from your heart, addressing God with them in complete frankness and love as if you are standing before Him, seeing Him.

Whenever you are fought with lukewarmness, and also at the times of your spiritual fervor, practice these private prayers and see the result on your life.

Break free from the concepts of quantity, speed, routine and law of your prayers. Try to pray with spirit, with understanding and with emotion. Do the same regarding the other spiritual practices but beware of falling down. If you feel lukewarm, pray a smaller number of prayers but more deeply. Then try to reach the same number of prayers with the same depth. If you are not able, go on with the same small number because the depth is more important and it cures you of lukewarmness.

Lukewarmness is not confined to prayers, reading, meditation and other spiritual practices but it may attack the inner feelings of the heart, the various fruits of the spirit and the spiritual life as a whole. Perhaps the holy zeal for ministry has become less fervent than before, the longing for consecration has weakened, or the zealous condemnation of oneself and leading a life of repentance have become less powerful. etc.

Also some signs of lukewarmness can in themselves be a cause for lukewarmness. Some examples of this are:
- Absorbing oneself in matters not relating to God. This may be said to be a sign or a cause for lukewarmness.
- Being satisfied with a certain level and not improving oneself can also be regarded as a cause and a sign.
- Falling from love to routine, which we discussed in this chapter as being a sign of lukewarmness, can be regarded also as a cause.

We now need to discuss causes and remedies.

The Causes Of Lukewarmness And The Remedy

+Being occupied with matters not related to God.

One of the most dangerous causes of lukewarmness is to being occupied in such a way that a person cannot find time for God or for their spiritual life. As a result, the spiritual practices which make the heart fervent are lost and one becomes lukewarm.

Preoccupations vary; some of which are worldly and some are in the field of religious ministry. A person may be preoccupied with family affairs, a certain study or activity, a certain amusement, with a hobby or some work to the extent that they cannot find time for their spiritual practices. We give such a person two pieces of advice:

1. You need regulate your time (setting priorities).

2. Remember the verse which says, *"For what is a man profited if he gains the whole world, and loses his own soul?"* *(Matt.·16:16).*

And in order to regulate your time in such a way that you give part of your time to spiritual matters, you have to recognize the value of spiritual practices for your life and the value of your eternity. If you came to know this, you would be concerned about it and would allocate some time to your spiritual practices, however busy you may be.

Beware being overly involved in matters relating to the ministry and the church, for this would hinder you in such a way that pleases your conscience yet could keep you lukewarm.

Know well that if your spiritual life weakens, your ministry will accordingly weaken and yield no fruit. Ministry is not just an activity but it is a spirit transferred from one person to another, it is a life which the person ministered to absorbs from the minister. Know also that being overly preoccupied in church service is not an excuse for a weak relationship with God. God does not require from yon a service which may drive you away from prayers and meditation and from a secret life with Him. You need then to organize your ministry.

Remember the story of the elder son who said to his father, *"Lo, these many years I have been serving you, ... and yet you never gave me a young goat, that I might make merry with my friends."* *(Luke 15:29)*. In spite of the long service of that son, his will was opposed to his father's will and he was spiritually weak. This was revealed by the way he talked with his father, his opinion concerning his brother and that he would not share his father's joy for the return of the lost son.

Do not be like that elder son whose service detained him from enjoying his father's love and from giving care to himself and to his spirituality.
Try to accept only responsibilities within your power and ability. For the sake of your spirituality, limit your activities. You will find many things that can be given up easily, such as some entertainment, socialising and useless chatter.

At least, try to raise your heart to God every now and then even though you are occupied all the time. Do not let any preoccupation take all your heart, or all your time because you do not have time to waste. Where is the time that belongs to God?

I do not want to tell you that God owns all your life. Amidst all your occupations, I would like you to remember two important points concerning God's share in your time:

1. Remember the Lord's Day to keep it holy.

2. Remember the commandment of the first fruits with regard to your time.

I know that if you are faithful concerning the commandment of the Lord's Day, you would have a spiritual stock to protect you from lukewarmness throughout the week.

If you were faithful concerning the commandment of the first fruits also and gave the first fruit of your day to God, then the fervor you gain from this would remain with you all the day long and encourage you to allocate other times to your spiritual practices.

Another point I would like to draw your attention to is, if you become occupied all day with worldly affairs, they will possess you and dominate over your heart and mind so that when you stand for prayer after that, your mind will be distracted with such matters and your prayer becomes weak. So, when we speak about preoccupations as a cause of lukewarmness, we do not mean only occupation of the time but also occupation of the mind and the heart. This is more dangerous because it goes into oneself. Hence, the church arranged for us the seven prayers of the hours in order that we may stop for part of the day and fill it with communion with God.

The church, in arranging these prayers, was careful that every three hours, a person would raise their heart to God and talk to Him away from all occupations and cares of life. By doing this a person would keep their spiritual fervor. So if you were faithful in performing the church arranged prayers you would not become lukewarm.

Among the causes of lukewarmness is being remote from God for a long time. Persons who are exposed to this are those who pray the matins (the first hour prayer) and the compline (prayer before sleeping) and nothing in between. These 'between' hours are usually busy, full of challenges, wars and offences.

If you want to escape lukewarmness, raise your heart to God every now and then even if with only one sentence or a short prayer that would only take just a minute or even a few seconds.

+ Being away from repentance.

Two types of people are fervent in spirit:

1. The first is a person who has recently repented and is humble and humiliated; their tears are ready in their eyes and they want to compensate for the 'years eaten by the locusts'. Such a person strives with all fervor.

2. The second is a person who has attained divine love. Love in their heart is a glowing fire that fills it with spiritual fervor. This appears in their prayers, ministry and in any spiritual act they perform.

Unlike this is a person who is in an intermediate state, they are lukewarm.

They resemble the people of Israel in the wilderness. They are no longer coming out of the land of servitude seeking God's salvation and experiencing His wonders for them, nor have they reached Canaan, the land flowing with milk and honey. They are neither ablaze with repentance nor with love. They have not the fervor of the tax - collector who stood afar off and would not so much as raise his eyes to heaven (Luke 18:13), nor the fervor of St. John the Apostle who leant on the Lord's bosom in familiarity and love.

They are in between; They are lukewarm.

They long for the days when they wept for their sins but cannot find them. They are now involved in a formal worship which has no spirit nor depth. They pray and fast, read the Holy Bible, attend spiritual meetings, confesses and partake of the Holy Communion and are perhaps also ministers. Despite all this they find no motive for humility of the heart. They have become indifferent to sin and so their conscience stopped rebuking them and they no longer feel undeserving. They lost the tears and fervor of repentance but at the same time they perform all the spiritual practices without depth or love. They neither attained heaven nor earth. They are lukewarm!!

Such a person has to be attached to persons of high spirituality, whether through close relations with them or reading about them. In this way they would feel themselves as nothing and the feelings of repentance and humility would return and motivate them into fervent repentance. They may also proceed to spiritual practices which can give them strength and restore to them the fervor of spirit, or make them feel their weakness and inability to practice them deeply. So they will return once more to the life of repentance but this time on a different level.

They may train themselves to be spiritual in their prayers, fasting and in all other practices. This would bring them out of mere formality and make them come into a deep communion with God. At this stage, they can be frank with themselves, seeing that they don't pray, fast or read as they ought. Hence they feel that they must learn to pray anew; fast and read in a proper way. They will begin again a life of true repentance feeling that they ought to repent for their present formal worship. This would lead them to fervor in worship.

Perhaps their repentance might not have been established on a proper or a strong basis and this led them to lukewarmness. In this case, they would have to set aright the basis of their repentance in order to live in a true spiritual fervor.

Perhaps the temporal motive for repentance vanished and this made them fall into lukewarmness. So a person must establish their relation with God on the right basis, being on love of God and for good. They must also be convinced of the necessity of a spiritual life. This would remedy their lukewarmness.

The first motive for repentance is just a stage on a road. A truly repentant person must not stop at that stage but they have to correct their spiritual motives so that they may continue to be fervent.

Another cause for lukewarmness is:

+ Satisfaction and making no progress.

As long as the spiritual person progresses, they keep their spiritual fervor because movement implies fervor. If a person stops at a certain level, they become lukewarm. Many people face such a problem.

Those who were not used to praying before their repentance and then began to taste the sweetness of praying found a pleasure which filled their hearts with spiritual fervor. When they attained a certain level of prayer, they stopped there and in time their prayers became routine. By not striving further in prayer they became lukewarm.

This could also happen with regard to other spiritual practices whether fasting, reading or ministry.

They remind us of the car; as long as it moves, it keeps hot, but if it stops for a long time the battery grows weak and has to be charged.

Take as an example St. Paul the Apostle who was caught up to the third heaven (2 Cor. 12:2) but despite this he said, *"Not that I have already attained, or am already perfected; but I press on... (I press toward the goal) ...that I may lay hold of that..."* (Phil.3:12-14).

If a great Apostle like St. Paul strives and presses on, what ought you to do?

Pressing on makes you always unsatisfied to stop at any level you attain. So, you move again and thus you avoid falling into lukewarmness.

Stopping has its dangers for it does not only lead to lukewarmness but also may lead to falling into sin. Usually a person who stops does not only make no progress but is also liable to move backwards!

A spiritual life is a life of perpetual movement, perpetual fervor and perpetual progress. Its objective is to strive to attain fullness.

A believer must not be content to live in the spirit and according to the spirit but must strive to achieve the words of the Apostle, *"Be filled with the Spirit..." (Eph.5:18)*. This fullness keeps them from falling into lukewarmness. However, in spite of this progress and this fullness beware of another cause:

+ The danger of the best places.

A person, at the beginning of their spiritual life, lives in humility and therefore grace is always near to them because, *"The Lord is near to those who have a broken heart." (Ps.34:18)*.

Through humility and grace, they live spiritually fervent. But as such a person progresses, certain responsibilities are entrusted to them and they become leaders, having a position of authority. The position of authority is not dangerous in itself but if the persons heart is exalted and they become careless, losing their watchfulness and humility, they could fall into lukewarmness.

At the beginning of their repentance, a person enters the church saying, 'O Lord, I am not in harmony with this beautiful tune, I am out of place amidst this congregation of saints and I do not deserve to be in this holy place, *"I will come into Your house in the multitude of Your mercy;" (Ps.5:7)*.' But afterwards, they go to church in order to teach, to organize or to manage. They enter as a leader and forget how they used to feel before. They may also enter without awe, without kneeling and with no tears in their eyes, all which they used to do at the beginning! They may enter church to give orders, to rebuke or to discuss a certain system or manage a certain job. They may enter church to perform a certain ministry or activity they are responsible for; but in all this they may forget God and forget that they are in God's house. Of course, their previous words 'I am not in harmony with this beautiful tune' have vanished completely.

Perhaps this person will not stand during church prayers! The church has lost its awe in their sight and when they are there, they talk with this or that person, laugh with their friends and call whomever they want in a loud voice without any reverence for the place. The church prayers become to them mere musical tunes which they mastered and words which they know and even know their deep meaning. They are no longer a talk with God. Is there greater lukewarmness than this.

What raises wonder is that such a person may sometimes find excuses for such lukewarmness by saying that they have attained the love which casts out fear (1Jn. 4:18)!!

Be on your guard!! Do not consider yourself one of the pillars of the church nor feel that you are important and that if you were absent, you would leave an empty gulf which cannot not be filled.

Be on your guard also, in case you dispute with the persons responsible for the ministry, do not threaten to leave the ministry, thinking that this would shake the church foundations. Know that behind all this, there is a feeling of self-importance concealing behind it a hidden pride which is the actual cause of your lukewarmness.

If your lukewarmness has resulted in the above, the Lord may prevent you from ministry for some time to show you that the church can manage without you. This would humble you and restore your contrition; then your spiritual fervor would return to you again.

After the victory of Elijah, the Great Prophet on Mount Carmel where he defeated and removed the prophets of Baal and Asherah (1 Kings 18:20-40) and after the heavens had opened another time due to his prayers (1 Kings 18 41-45), he heard from the Lord this command, *"Go, return on your way... and Elisha the son of Shaphat ... you shall anoint as prophet in your place."* *(1Kings 19:15,16)*. Elisha was anointed and when Elijah was taken up he took a double portion of his spirit and performed many more miracles than Elijah as well. After Elijah was taken up the earth remained as it was and continued, however, this did not diminish the honour of that great prophet whom God glorified by lifting him up to heaven and by his appearance on the mount of transfiguration.

God has many arrows in His quiver and He is able to raise up children to Abraham from stones (Matt.3:9).

So, if God entrusts you with some ministry, say with Moses the great prophet, '0 Lord, who am I that you count me among those who minister to You while I am slow of speech and of a slow tongue' (Ex. 4:10). Also, 'I may be a stumbling block for the ministry or negligent towards its responsibilities. Certainly You have many ministers who are better than me. You only encourage me by employing me in your vineyard though I am undeserving.'

With such a humble spirit, you ought to behave in the best places in order that you may not become lukewarm. If people praise you, remember your sins and weak points. Beware not to accept any praise or let it enter into yourself lest grace should forsake you and you quench your fervor. You should rather attribute all glory to God and say with St. Paul the humble, *"But by the grace of God I am what I am." (1 Cor.15:10).*

If you come to the best places as a leader, put before you an important rule, which is:

Be careful not to turn from being a worshipper into being a scholar.
Be careful not to seek knowledge just for its own sake nor to become a source of knowledge.

Amidst intellectual matters you may neglect the spirit!

You may be allured by books and by reading and forget yourself and your eternity.

Be careful not to be allured by argument and become so involved in it that you fall in numerous quarrels and lose your love for others. Your concern becomes to win the argument and conquer the others.

Perhaps you would exalt yourself while arguing with others, or hurt, injure or ridicule them. Or you would have self-confidence concerning whatever you say or hold to your opinion and refuse to yield.

Be careful not to refuse any objection to your views or any argument against them. Also be careful not to speak haughtily.

Such modes of argument, even though in the field of dogma,

would make you fall into spiritual lukewarmness. You may win the debate reasonably but lose yourself spiritually and you may even lose both. Many people have become a store for knowledge but their spirit remains empty.

Little knowledge with more practical application is far more important than to have a vast amount of knowledge without practical experience. You may be careful to read a certain number of chapters of the Holy Bible each day yet without deep understanding, meditation, application and without prayer and so you get no spiritual benefit. Thus our life remains lukewarm.

So it is not important how much we read but that we read spiritually and with depth.

Do not take the best positions/services nor seek it, whether it be administrative, scientific or leadership. Consider yourself small and do not claim to have knowledge of everything. There is nothing wrong with saying humbly that you do not know.

Another cause for lukewarmness can be the effect of others in your life.

+ The others in your life.

It is dangerous to make people the aim of your spiritual life instead of God.

At the beginning you live a spiritual life putting before you your eternity and motivated by your love for God but as you make progress, others enter your life and become part of your aims. The main objective of your spirituality may become the attempt to be an example for others or to avoid offences. In such a case, you do good not out of love for good or for God... but to be an example for people, to become a model of the spiritual life, or as a light for those who walk in the darkness.

For the same reason, you avoid sinning in order not to be a stumbling block for them, not out of hatred for sin. You may even slacken in resisting sin secretly as long as you do not offend anyone.

So your spiritual motive is external not coming from within you and so you become lukewarm. You may even develop a double nature, one for when you are with or in front of people and the other away from people, in secret.

You may become anxious about how people regard or judge what you say or do. You may go as far as to do what would please people and little by little their opinions become your only concern. Here the spiritual objective is lost and your spiritual life becomes lukewarm.

For example, when you pray in a meeting, you may be interested in the opinion of people concerning your prayer and so your prayer is said for the sake of people not for God's sake. Tears may even come with your prayer not out of love for God but in order that people may praise your spirituality in prayers or that you may be content with yourself. In all this, God is not present in your life. Know then that people differ in opinion as mother Sarah the nun says, 'If I seek to please everyone, I would lose my way knocking at every door'.

How easy it is for people to think of accuracy as excess. Would we then be inaccurate in order to please them?

Your life may become lukewarm also due to paying many compliments to others. For their sake, you may waste much time in things of no benefit. For their sake you may take part in troublesome talks and discussions. For their sake your prayers and meditations may be delayed. Listen. then to the deep words of St. Paul the Apostle, *"Do I seek to please men? For if I still pleased men, I would not be a servant of Christ." (Gal.1:10)*.

So let your relations with people be within the spiritual scope so that you may not become lukewarm in spirit.

+ Neglecting spiritual practices and prayers of the hours.

Nearly every case of lukewarmness in one's spiritual life is due, among other reasons, to neglecting the spiritual practices and the prayers of the hours. That is because such practices remind a person of God, motivates them to spiritual actions and strengthens their heart. So if a person neglects these they become weak and lukewarm.

By spiritual practices we mean; prayer, reading, meditation, fasting, confession, Holy Communion, spiritual meetings, attending church regularly and ministry. But, they must be practiced in a spiritual way.

Perhaps, one would ask, 'Though I practice all such means, I am lukewarm. What is the reason and what is the remedy?'.

The answer is:

1-. You practice them routinely, in the wrong way. In this case you ought to practice them with understanding, emotion, concentration and spirit.

2. You are passing through an external war. In this case patience is necessary till God delivers you from such a war or helps you to overcome it. Besides, you must go on with the spiritual work.

Falling in lukewarmness with regard to spiritual practices ought not to make you stop performing them. This would make you fall more instead of helping you improve yourself.

One of the most important spiritual means (practices) is the prayers of the hours (The Canonical Hours, the Agbia). When a person does them consistently, their conscience may be affected by some words which gives them spiritual fervor. If they are not affected at the time of the prayer, then this may happen later.

For example, the compline prayer reminds a person of death, condemnation and eternity. The Midnight Prayer calls a person to awake and repent. The vespers prayer reminds us of our sins and to be vigilant, calling us to repent and ask forgiveness. The Prime reminds a person that they ought to walk in the spirit throughout the day and to begin well. The other prayers also have a spiritual effect. So if the person pays attention to the meaning while praying, their conscience will certainly remain alert.

If a person is not affected by these prayers, they will be in due time and they need to be patient. The person can say in their prayer, *"My soul waits for the Lord more than those who watch for the morning..."* (Ps. 130:6).

Another cause for lukewarmness is:

+ Thinking that the spiritual life is mere practices.

Some people think that a spiritual life are only prayers, fasting, confession, communion, meetings and ministry. They plan a schedule for their practices and try to carry them out to comfort their conscience but by doing so they fall into lukewarmness. What is the reason then?

The reason is that they confine themselves to such practices and neglect the purity of the heart within which is the actual basis for the spiritual act and without which one becomes lukewarm.

Mere spiritual practices without the fruit of the Spirit within may make the person proud like the Pharisee. In this case a person becomes like a sepulcher, white from outside while their hearts were void of true spiritual feelings.

Be concerned then with the internal work and with the main virtues such as love, faith, humility, meekness, purity and chastity. Then your prayer will rise like a flame out of a pure heart full of love for God and for virtues.

Someone may stand to pray while they are upset or holding a grudge against someone. They may also pray, read, preach or teach and their heart is full of anger, fury, pride and so on. How would their prayer be fervent while their heart is void of spirit. How would they be attached to God in prayer while their heart is away from God due to rage, meanness and contention?

So, if you want to get rid of lukewarmness, be careful to make your spiritual action based on the fruit of the Spirit within you (Gal. 5:22).

In all your practices, remember that the Lord admonishes you expressly saying, *"My son give me your heart..." (Prov. 23:26)* and rebukes the Jews saying, *"When you spread out your hands, I will hide My eyes from you; even though you make many prayers, I will not hear. Your hands are full of blood. (Is.1:15).*

This leads us to another point.

+ A sin or a lust in one's life.

A person may walk along the spiritual path in a proper way for some time and then some lust or love of sin begins to occupy their heart and feelings, competing in them with God. When this happens, they may become lukewarm.

When one's heart is overcome by sin it has left it's 'first love', God and this affects its spiritual fervor.

Search then, what strange thing occupies God's place in your heart. What is the sin which has crept into you whether it is plain or concealed and whether it comes in sheep's' clothing or in the guise of a virtue to deceive you!

Sin may be disguised in the form of a virtue like zeal, defending the truth and love for reform, if such things are done without discernment or understanding!

A person may dispute with people and be in enmity with them, rebukes and reproaches them unmercifully, without love or understanding under the pretext of defending the truth and in the name of reform. They may criticize, condemn and even insult others. They may become harsh and turn into a fire which devours whatever it meets. They develop a critical eye which sees only what is bad and finds nothing good in people. Doubts everyone and accuses everyone falsely. Such a person pretends to gather up the tares but in fact they themselves have become a tare. They search for their spirituality but don't find it and they are lukewarm. The Lord refers to them when He says, *"...I will spew you out of My mouth." (Rev.3:16).*

This does not mean that a person has to refrain from any act of reform, showing zeal or defending the truth but they ought to do this with understanding and wisdom in a spiritual way as the Holy Bible says, *"Let all that you do be done with love." (1Cor. 16:14)* and also, *"Who is wise and understanding among you? Let him show by good conduct that his works are done in the meekness of wisdom. But if you have bitter envy and self-seeking in your hearts, do not boast and lie against the truth. This wisdom does not descend from above..." (James 3:13-15).*

This is the spirit of reform, in love and meekness with wisdom. In this way a person will not sin in their zeal and will not become lukewarm in spirit.

Beautiful are the words of the Apostle concerning reforming others, *"...you who are spiritual restore such a one in a spirit of gentleness, considering yourself lest you also be tempted. Bear one another's burdens..." (Gal.6:1,2).*

I draw your attention to the fact that many began their repentance in such a spiritual fervor that people admired them and nominated them for the ministry. Then in ministry, they had a zeal for God but not according to knowledge (Rom. 10:2) and so they lost fervor and became lukewarm!

In fact, occupying oneself solely to reforming others has

destroyed many persons!! A person who wants to reform others, thinks all the time of others sins and forgets their own and so they slacken. At the beginning of their repentance they concentrated on their spiritualties and on their own salvation but in the ministry they forgot themselves completely and were wholly concerned with the salvation of others or with their sins or with reforming society! They do not even do this in a proper way but in a manner void of love and perhaps concealing inner pride!

If such a person would ask about the cause of their lukewarmness, we would answer that it is due to their conduct! It would have been better for them if they had lived in humility seeking only their own salvation. Such a person should consider that they also are sinners who need reform instead of being concerned with others and their faults and with those who become lukewarm in spirit.

Another word I whisper in your ear which may be the cause of your lukewarmness and your faults while trying to reform others out of zeal; Perhaps you have cruelty of which you are not aware. When you began your life with God, this cruelty crept stealthily into you and began to appear in your zeal and reformation in the name of God!

Look to St. Paul the Apostle, who said to his disciple St. Timothy the Bishop, *"...convince, rebuke, exhort..." (2 Tim. 4:2),* how he himself used to reform! He addressed the priests of Ephesus whom he called saying, *"...remember that for three years I did not cease to warn everyone night and day with tears..." (Acts 20:31).* St Paul never became lukewarm because he warned them with tears. In those tears there was gentleness and love.

As cruelty is one of the causes of lukewarmness, condemning others is another cause. In both cases, grace forsakes the person to humble them by making them feel the pain of their actions (James 5:17). Forsaken by grace, one falls into lukewarmness.

For spiritual fervor is not a human act but the act of the Spirit within oneself. So when a person by their misconduct quenches the Spirit they become lukewarm.

Another similar reason is pride.

+ Pride.

Pride is of many kinds.

To start with, we remember the words of the Holy Bible, *"Pride goes before destruction, and a haughty spirit before a fall." (Prov. 16:18).* If pride leads to destruction and a fall, then it would definitely lead to lukewarmness.

An example of pride is when a person thinks that they have achieved their aim and so they slacken by not continuing to strive! It is like a person who takes a train with a strong longing to arrive at their destination. When they arrive, the strong desire leaves them.

There are others who although they do all things that they are commanded to do, say in humility, *"We are unprofitable servants..."(Luke 17:10).* Such persons would not become lukewarm because they are always longing to achieve their aim. Whatever perfection they attain they say, *"Not that I have already attained... but I press on that I may lay hold... forgetting those things which are behind and reaching forward to those things which are ahead." (Phil.3:12,13).*

This striving gives fervor which dismisses lukewarmness. A person who strives whenever they advance, feels that their previous life, however elevated it was, was nothing but lukewarmness. This attitude motivates them to continue to strive and to be more fervent.

The other kind of pride is when a person feels that they are better and more important than others. They think that others ought to treat them as superiors, with respect, be submissive and obey whatever they want.

At the beginning of their repentance, they felt humble and undeserving but now, due to their pride, grace forsakes them and so they become lukewarm in order that they may feel their weakness and be humbled.

Spiritual fervor never comes while there is pride. If it happens that either of them finds the other somewhere it says to the other what Abraham said to Lot, *"Please separate from me. If you take the left, then I will go to the right, or, if you go to the right, then I will go to the left." (Gen.13:9).*

However, those who are endowed with mental or spiritual talents, may begin well but are fought afterwards and become lukewarm.

So, God, in His love for mankind, does not give His gifts to everyone, because not all people can endure such gifts!! Some may be exalted in their hearts and become lukewarm!

True are the words of one of the fathers in this concern, he said,

'If God gives you a gift (talent), ask Him to give you together with it, humility so that you may be able to endure it and if God doesn't, ask him to take it away.'

See also the beautiful words of David the Prophet, *"It is good for me that I have been afflicted, that I may learn Your statutes." (Ps. 119:71).* He says also, *"The Lord is near to those who have a broken heart." (Ps. 34:18).*

So be humble and humiliated so that God may be near to you and gives you a fervent spirit and by such you will not become lukewarm.

Let us move now to another cause.

<u>+ The quick transition from the life of repentance to the life of rejoicing.</u>

At the beginning when one repents a person is often humiliated and humble, often shedding tears for their sins. Others may advise this person to stop this sorrow because the Lord Jesus Christ has already forgiven their sins and encourages them to rejoice! If the repentant at this advice, stops being humble, they may lose their spiritual fervor and become lukewarm.

Any sin which one does not resist with due humility and humiliation, may return. At the lease they would become mindless of the sin and become lukewarm.

St. Paul the Apostle for example, with all his spiritual greatness, never stopped humbling himself and never forgot his sins but used to say, *"For I am the least of the apostles, who am not worthy to be called an apostle, because I persecuted the church of God." (1Cor. 15:9).*

David the Prophet also after he sinned and repented and was promised forgiveness, put his sin always before him (Ps.51) and all night he drenched his couch with his tears (Ps.6).

As St. Paul and David, the Prophet kept their hearts' humble, they also kept their spiritual fervor and avoided becoming lukewarm.

Do not hasten then to a life of joy but rather if you found joy say, 'I do not deserve it!', or at least be humble of heart even though you experience the joy of the spirit.

Another cause for lukewarmness is our next point.

+ Slackening and leniency.

It is obvious that these two causes lead to lukewarmness. They are against spiritual striving and hinder the spiritual path to perfection. If a person succumbs to them, they affect their prayers and watchfulness and hinders their effort to restraint, even by force.

The Kingdom of God shall not be given to those who are lazy but to those who strive and the Holy Bible says, *"Cursed is he who does the work of the Lord deceitfully." (Jer. 48:10).*

+ Conclusion.

In conclusion, we say that the subject of lukewarmness is vast and needs much more to be said on it. But I shall stop here and return to it again in another book, God willing.

CHAPTER 12

WAR OF SADNESS

What is sadness? What are its signs and causes? What are it results and what is its remedy? We shall discover this and show the difference between profitable sadness and harmful sadness, whether it is a war or a disease.

Holy Sadness

No doubt there is holy sadness, motivated by spiritual motives. The person subject to this kind of sadness behaves in a spiritual way. This kind of sadness is also temporary not a way of life.

An example of this is Nehemiah who on hearing that the wall of Jerusalem was broken down, its gates were burned with fire and its people were in great distress and reproach, said, *"I sat down and wept and mourned for many days; I was fasting and praying before the God of heaven." (Neh. 1:4).* King Artaxerxes observed his sadness and said to him, *"This is nothing but sorrow of heart..."* and Nehemiah answered the king, *"Why should my face not be sad, when the city, the place of my fathers' tombs lies waste and its gates are burned with fire?" (Neh. 2:2,3).*

This sadness motivated Nehemiah to pray and fast and to carry out an effective positive work and this ended his sadness and the whole people rejoiced with great joy (Neh. 12:43).

A similar example is Ezra the Prophet, who upon seeing the transgressions of the people, was sad and his sadness led him to fast and pray. He succeeded in making the people confess and present offerings for their trespasses and so overcame his sadness. (Ez. 9,10).

Other examples can be found in stories from 'The Paradise of

The Holy Fathers', which describes the many tears of the father saints. In this book we also read the famous advice which says, 'Sit in your cell and weep for your sins'.

We read also about the sadness which accompanies repentance and helps a person to be humble and lowly of heart.

Some examples of this are; fasting in (Joel 2:12-17), the fast of the people of Nineveh and how they humbled themselves before God, covering themselves in sackcloth and ashes (Jonah 3) and the repentance of David and how he drenched his couch with his tears (Ps. 6).

The sadness of repentance usually ends in joy and inner comfort within the heart. It led them to correct their ways as a whole. Perhaps this is what was meant in the Holy Bible by the words, *"…by a sad countenance the heart is made better." (Eccl. 7:3).*

We also hear about sadness in the field of ministry as St. Paul the Apostle says, *"We are hard pressed on every side, yet not crushed." (2Cor. 4:8).* Thus, sadness in the field of ministry was accompanied by comfort as St. Paul also says, *"God… who comforts us in all our tribulation, that we may be able to comfort those who are in any trouble" (2Cor. 1:4).*

One of the most wonderful examples of holy sadness is that of our Lord Jesus Christ in the Garden of Gethsemane when He began to be sorrowful and deeply distressed and said, *"My soul is exceedingly sorrowful, even to death." (Matt. 26:37,38).*

Another example is in the Lamentations of Jeremiah which are all prophecies about the Lord Jesus Christ.

The Lord spoke to His disciples about sadness saying, *"Therefore you now have sorrow; but I will see you again and your heart will rejoice, and your joy no one will take from you." (Jn. 16:22).*

So we learn that holy sadness is due to spiritual reasons and is usually accompanied by comfort and hope and it ends with joy. It is also temporary, not prolonged.

Natural Sadness

An example of this kind ·is sadness for the death of a loved one, like that of Mary and Martha who wept at the tomb of Lazarus.

Another example is the sadness of Job after the death of his sons and daughters, the destruction of his house and the loss of his health.

Jacob also wept when he heard that a beast had devoured his son Joseph (Gen. 37:34).

This is natural sadness but there is another kind and it is our next point.

Wrong Sadness And Its Causes

Wrong sadness is that which involves sin, such as:

1. The sadness of some person for not recognizing a certain sinful lust in their heart.

An example of this is the sadness of King Ahab who went into his house sullen and displeased because he could not take possession of the vineyard of Naboth the Jezreelite (1Kings 21:4). His sadness led him to kill, oppress and lie so that he might attain his desire.

2. Sadness due to jealousy and envy.

An example of this is the sadness of the elder son who refused to enter the house to share his father's joy for the return of his brother and said to his father, *"...you never gave me a young goat, that I might make merry with my friends. But as soon as this son of yours came... you killed the fatted calf for him." (Luke 15:28-30).*

An example of jealous sadness is when a person feels that another one has obtained something which they think they have more right to.

3. Sadness due to failure.

Sadness is not a remedy for failure but the remedy is to find the reasons of the failure and to remedy them in a positive way. Mere sadness adds to failure another problem that needs a solution.

This kind of sadness becomes more dangerous if it is due to failure to commit a certain sin. Some examples of this are: Amnon's initial failure to commit sin with his sister Tamar (2 Sam. 13); Ahab's initial failure to take possession of Naboth' vineyard; the failure of any student to cheat in exams or the failure of any person to take revenge for the murder of one of their relatives. It is failure to commit some sin and being sad for it is another sin.

4. Sadness caused by despair.

An example of this is the despair of Esau when he knew that his brother stole their father's blessing and there was no hope to get it back, as his father Isaac said to him, *"Your brother came with deceit and has taken away your blessing.. Indeed I have made him your master... What shall I do now for you, my son?"* When Esau heard the words of his father, he cried with an exceedingly great and bitter cry and he lifted up his voice and wept (Gen. 27:33-38).

5. Sadness due to a tribulation that appears to have no solution or no end.

As a remedy, a person in such a state has to say with David the prophet, *"Why are you cast down, O my soul? And why are you disquieted within me? Hope in God." (Ps. 42:11).*

Do not heap up the problems before you and stand in sadness seeking no solution, having no hope and failing to trust God. Remember that the Holy Bible says, *"...lest you sow as others who have no hope." (1 Thess. 4:13).*

Sadness without hope is wrong even if its cause is natural, such as weeping for the death of someone or for a spiritual reason like weeping for committing some sin.

If problems/tribulations encompass you, disperse them and put God between you and them so they disappear and God appears with His help.

6. Sadness caused by excessive sensitivity.

There may be someone who is very sensitive concerning their dignity or their rights. They may get annoyed for any reason, for the slightest reason or even for no reason. They want to be treated in a special way, very gently, carefully and leniently. If they are not treated so and this rarely happens, of course they will be sad.

7. Sadness of those who escape from reality, refusing it and making for themselves an imaginary substitute that cannot be attained. Such persons rebel and refuse their conditions but do not try to change them in a practical way which would resolve for them what they want. They are content with their rebelliousness and continue as they are; sad and resentful of everything.

If they sometimes feel happy, that would be through some daydreams which they live in imagining things which they desire. But they wake up from their dreams and imaginary world to find themselves where they were and so become even more resentful and sad.

We advise those persons to be realistic, either live content and happy, satisfied and thankful for what they have or try to change their real conditions in a practical way and not remain sad.

8. Sadness because of being ill-tempered and intolerant.

An open-hearted and broad-minded person can overlook many things and let them melt in their but those who do not endure are liable to be sad. Broad-mindedness is also a remedy for sadness. Instead of being sad, a broad-minded person thinks of solutions.

An intelligent person, when faced with some problem or trouble, tries to find a solution for it instead of being anxious and depressed. When they find a solution, they rejoice and the problem loses it seriousness. If they do not find a solution, they wait patiently. A person who cannot be patient is no doubt ill-tempered and their sadness increases because they feel helpless.

9. Sadness due to an external war waged by an adversary for no apparent reason.
The devil may cause trouble which they may even invent or they may magnify trivial things which in fact do not lead to sadness, or trifle with the person, whenever he finds the person pleased with a certain position, he entices him with other positions as if they were better, but when the person attains such new positions, he entices him with others or with the first. The opponent wants by this to lead a person to hesitation and instability so that they may become sad.

For example, when he finds a monk living in solitude, he entices him to go and serve in ministry where there are crowns prepared for those who participate in building the Kingdom. And if a monk has a certain ministry, the devil entices him with solitude, a life of meditation and perpetual prayers, enjoying an uninterrupted life in God's presence. By these temptations the devil keeps the monk in doubt about his vocation and so he becomes sad.

Doubt is another cause for sadness.

10. If doubt lasts, it will destroy the soul and lead it to sadness and anxiety.

A person may doubt the honesty of some friend, or the faithfulness and chastity of their husband/wife or doubt God's protection and help. Doubt may be directed against faith or against the way of life the person is leading, whether it is according to God's will or not! A person may doubt also that there is a certain plot against them, though they do not know what it is.

The source of doubtful thoughts is the mind. They are intended to cause suffering and lead a person to wrong behavior.

For example, the husband who doubts the chastity of his wife, shuts the doors and windows and spies on her. He gives himself the right to examine her letters and draws and questions her concerning everything she does. All his doubts end up tormenting her and she may be completely innocent. He censures her for every smile and for every word, for every meeting and for every motion. Both their lives turn into a hell and sadness here leads to serious results.

Sadness is a known and famous war.

Let us move now to a fourth kind of sadness.

Sickness As A Result Of Sadness

Doubt leading to sadness may develop into a sickness and sadness also may turn into a sickness.

In the case of sadness, thoughts press on a person and affect their spirit and lose their cheerfulness.

A sad thought sticks to the person like an illness and does not leave them. It accompanies them while they are sitting, walking or sleeping with dark thoughts full of distress, anxiety and fear. It paints a sad picture and hopeless scenarios.

Such sadness destroys a person's life and spirituality, their soul and mind, convincing them that they are lost and there is no hope....

For example, someone may think that their sin will not be forgiven and that their sin is blasphemy against the Holy Spirit (Matt.12:31). Perhaps it is the devil who put this thought in their mind to make them become sad and in their despair, they are convinced that they have lost their eternity, seeing no way for salvation.

The devil may also lead them to the same thought and the same sadness by reminding them of the words said about Esau, *"...he found no place for repentance, though he sought it diligently with tears." (Heb.12:17)*.

While the devil is highlighting verses that make us sad he also hides all the verses that tell about God's acceptance of sinners, such as; *"The one who comes to Me I will by no means cast out." (Jn. 6:37)* and *"God our Savior, who desires all men to be saved and to come to the knowledge of the truth." (1 Tim. 2:4)*.

The devil may also present to him the verse that says, *"And I gave her time to repent of her sexual immorality, and she did not repent." (Rev. 2:21)*. By this, the devil intends to make the person feel that repentance has a fixed time and that time has passed by. Thus he removes every hope of salvation. David the Prophet must have experienced this when he wrote, *"Many are they who say of me "There is no help for him in God." (Ps. 3:2).*

The devil puts before the person the words, *"For it is impossible for those... to renew them again to repentance."* It is the way of the devil, to discard hope and make people fall in sadness and despair.

Of course, the above verses have an explanation but such a person needs someone to explain to them what they really mean. They need someone to tell them about God's boundless love and how He accepted the thief at the last moments of his life.

The sadness of a despairing person is not the kind of sad countenance which makes the heart better (Eccl. 7:3).

Another cause of this type of sadness may be the feeling of guilt, as in the case of someone who loses their father or son and feels that they are the cause of their death. This troubles them and makes them continuously sad. They convince themselves saying, 'Perhaps I neglected caring for him and if I had not neglected him he would not have died.' The devil keeps on reminding them of a certain occasion on which they were negligent. If anyone tried to convince them that they did not neglect and that they did everything they could, they would argue, from their sadness, 'Perhaps if I had called in a more famous physician he would not have died.' Etc. Thus they become overwhelmed by such sad thoughts.

Sadness may be due to a disease which they believe that cannot be cured.

Such sadness causes the person to be anxious about every medical examination and medical test.

Many are the causes which lead to this sadness which can cause sickness. A person cannot get rid of such sadness nor give themselves the chance to be healed of it.

The Symptoms And Their Remedy

A person who has the sadness sickness is always melancholy, with sad countenance and features, often weeping, often complaining, despairing and crushed by negative thoughts and has no hope. They think that they have lost their eternity, have destroyed themselves and their career, have lost their health or that they were the cause of destroying another person or that what awaits them is worse than what has passed.

You may try to correct their thoughts but they refuse, looking at you in despair and weeping. What they hear from you they heard before but they found that it was in vain.

They may also refuse any discussion at all feeling that there is no use and that others do not sympathise with them.

While the person who does not suffer from sadness in this way, wants to talk about their troubles so that they may find a solution.

The problem with the negative sad person is that they either do not find a solution and so becomes sadder, or finds a person who comforts them and so they go to them frequently. They may spend long hours every time talking and arguing with that person who gives them comfort till that person tires from them and starts to avoid them. This would trouble them and lead them to feel that they have lost the heart which gave them comfort and so they sink deeper into sadness and sickness.

As to the remedy, there are two types of persons sick with sadness.

A) A type that refuses to be comforted and refuses any understanding.

B) A type that holds to their opinion. Though they are helped out of it, they return to it; and though they are healed they become sick again and probably to a worse degree.

The person with this degree of sadness may even contemplate suicide.

They think that by suicide they may get rid of their pains and distress. Then either they carry out the idea or find that it is also useless because they believe in eternity, or because they prefer sadness to death or because they try to find solutions for their problems through imagination, thoughts and daydreams.

In general sadness would eventually affect their health. Sad thoughts press on them leaving them exhausted and worn out in soul and body. They may be enclosed within one idea encompassing them in such a way that they find themselves unable to come out of it. It is a disease which troubles them and troubles those around them. They trouble their physician, their spiritual guide etc. Their father confessor becomes at a loss how to behave towards them.

What is the remedy then?

+ Sadness is not a remedy for your problems!

The first remedy is to believe with all your heart that sadness is not a remedy for your problems.

You may face some problem as all people may and this would cause distress in your heart or trouble but with you in particular, sadness lasts longer than it ought to until others observe that it is not natural sadness.

People may try to comfort you or relieve you but you refuse such comfort. This makes people avoid talking to you, which in turn makes you to be sadder and self-centered.

Here, let me ask you, 'Did your sadness benefit you anything? Did it solve your problem? Did it give you inner comfort? Or did it rather trouble you more? Did it make you more comfortable in your relations with others or make your relations worse? No doubt, you have lost more than you expected through sadness'.

In fact your sadness became a problem greater than that which you were sad for! At the same time, the first problem remained without a solution. The problem of your sadness has added to your problems that you have become self-centered and on bad terms with others. You lost the calmness which you lived in and revealed to others a defect which they were not aware of concerning you. That defect is that you are not long-suffering and have no ability to endure problems. Why allow all this negative affect in your life?

Be realistic and try to find solutions for your problems and do not be encompassed within sadness. If you do not find a solution, wait for the Lord or endure and live your life as it is.

If you feel sad due to human nature, do not let this sadness last long or continue. Do not reveal your feeling before others and do not let them look at you in compassion or in despair of your improvement.

Try to be stronger than the problem. If you are not able, present the problem before God, the most powerful, with whom all things are possible (Matt. 19:26), then leave it in His hands and think no longer of it.

There are many problems which can be solved through faith, submission and prayer but there isn't any problem that can be solved through sadness. So you have to believe that God exists and that He will certainly help because He is the Almighty who sees everything. Nothing escapes Him and He knows about your troubles more than you know yourself. He has more compassion upon you than you have upon yourself.

Since God cares for you, do not try to shoulder any troubles yourself but instead leave the whole matter in God's hands.

There are problems which you can solve. There are other problems which you cannot solve and these you should not dwell upon or forget. Forgetting these unsolvable problems is a solution. You may ask, 'But how can I forget?' How can I forget the problem which sticks in my mind more than my skin sticks to my flesh? I think over it all the time while I am sitting, or walking, alone or with others. I think of nothing else. When I read, my mind goes astray and I talk of nothing except it. It is for me like the breath which comes in and out, whether I am aware or not? Here I present you with a practical solution, being.

+ Involvement.

Keep always busy and flee from the thought; this sad thought within you.

You must be convinced that thinking of a problem causes you much harm: It harms you physically and psychologically. It irritates you and tires you. The problem increases and at the same time you do not find a solution. So forget this diseased thought and say to yourself frankly, 'This thought has brought me nothing but trouble and I gain nothing by dwelling on it'.

If you cannot always keep busy, get involved in anything which may remove this troublesome thought from you. Continuous work is useful for those who suffer sadness. They go on working till they feel tired and sleep in peace and their nerves calm down from the stress of the thought.

Work also makes a person feel that they can do something useful or to carry a responsibility. This gives them comfort and they are pleased to see the fruit of their work. During all this, the troublesome thought moves away.

However, there are some people who may refuse to work or avoid it in order to be free to think about their unsolvable problems!

A thing to be regretted is that thinking and dwelling on an unsolvable problem (it becomes a disease) has become of great importance to some people to the extent that they cannot dispense with it. They want to think over the problem all the time and revolve in this endless circle to reach no solution! If such persons accept to work, it would be a healthy sign. It would be a sign that they accept to leave off the thought even for a little time, the time

230

of work. Their mere acceptance to work is useful even though they force themselves to do it. They will have improved when they accept to work with satisfaction and joy, finding pleasure in doing it.

Sometimes these types of compulsive worries refuse to work because they are unable to concentrate and it affects their physical ability to work! This excuse may be true with some people only. There may be a psychological factor behind this. For example, a person may feel a sudden physical weakness whenever they are given some work. This may be a reaction to their inner wish to refuse work.

Anyhow, one must accept work within one's capacity only or gradually according to the measures of such a sad person and according to their response to work. It is better also to give them the chance to choose the kind of work that suits them the most.

If such a person cannot do manual work, there are other activities which they may be able to take up. There are also various means of amusement and entertainment or reading that can occupy their mind. Another remedy is music.

+ Music.

No doubt there are certain kinds of music which have a strong effect on the soul. Such kinds of music can give comfort and calmness and can take a person away from sadness and distress.

One can choose a useful piece of music, which is not harmful spiritually, which has depth and can positively affect painful feelings, opening before one the doors of hope.

Here, I remember a daughter, Dr. Nabila Michael, who obtained a Masters and Doctorate in the field of treating people with music. She presented scientific research in this field which were esteemed by the university and other various organisations.

I think a sad person would not refuse to hear music. Music is not confined to singing because there is deep music not accompanied by singing. Religious music also affects the soul deeply. Of course, sad music must be avoided here because it may keep the sick person in pain, distress and reclusive.

Music is a remedy for the self within, for the feelings and emotions. In many cases it may be more effective than preaching and sermons. Certain spiritual songs and hymns can have this effect sometimes.

However, some people may seek remedy in chemical treatment through medicine. I shall present here my opinion concerning this kind of treatment comparing it with psychological and spiritual treatment.

+ Drugs and psychological treatment.

Treating with medicine may be acceptable when the sick person is in a certain nervous condition or is psychologically unable to accept any understanding or argument or is strongly sticking to their attitude. In such a case they are given medicine to calm them down so they can accept psychological treatment.

A person may be in such an agitated state that exhausts them and their nerves and physically affects them so violently that they cannot endure it. Much thinking may also stop them from sleeping. Such a person, suffering like this, is in urgent need for some rest. In such cases, the person is given some medicines as sedatives for relief.

In cases medicine may be necessary especially for a violent sick person who refuses to admit that they are sick and refuses any remedy.

However, we are aware of the various harms of medication and their effect on health but in such difficult cases, a physician can find no remedy other than medication. In spite of this I say expressly Medication must not be a continuous remedy or the only remedy. Psychological remedy is far better if done at the right time.

A sick person may take tranquilizers, sedatives or sleeping tablets to be relieved of the thought which troubles them. They may calm down and sleep but when they wake up or come to themselves, they find the thought still in their mind. So they take another dose and the circle goes on.

The medicine may bring no good result, so the sick person would be given a larger dose or other types of medication so that they may not get used to the first one or given a stronger medicine instead of the sedative.

Due to the excess of sleeping tablets, they may gain weight, or their mind may get weak and they may always feel dizzy or such and despite all this the troublesome thought continues.
Now let me tell you an important fact; Medication may be fit as a remedy for the symptoms of stress but they do not resolve your worries.

The causes are the thoughts and feelings which led to sadness and these thoughts affect the psyche, mind or soul.

What can medication do for all this?

Even if the medicine can cure one thing, they may destroy another. Medicines can make the sick person forget a troublesome thought, they may affect their memory as a whole.

A psychological treatment may work on the causes of sadness if applied in a deeper way but the problem is that psychological treatment needs a long time.

The patient wants to empty all that is within them and to tell all that troubles them. This may take long hours while the physician has no time for this. The sick person may also get used to talk for a long time and tell endless tales, so the physician gets bored and fears that the patient is wasting their time. This weariness of the physician makes them unable to listen any longer and the treatment stops.

In such a situation we cannot blame the physician for they may have an excuse especially if the sick person repeats the same stories or the same complaints which the physician made an effort in commenting on. The physician may be of the opinion that coddling the patient is not useful but would rather do them harm or encourage them to extend their meeting with the physician. It may also create a kind of familiarity between the patient and the physician and so they call for them continuously, during work and outside work.

No doubt the psychological treatment needs a long time, needs patience and forbearance as well as wisdom and knowledge of the human soul.

A physician may find that the doubts of the patient are not true and that the causes which they think have caused their trouble are exaggerated or imaginary or completely untruthful. Though the physician explains this to the sad person, they insist on their own thoughts and may also suspect the physician and their efficiency and faithfulness! It is a disease!

Sadness thus changes from its being an internal or external war to a disease.

We must examine all this in order to treat it. We present another remedy which is the spiritual remedy but before speaking about it I must discuss an important point which is sick piety.

+ Sickness caused by improper Piety.

Sick piety has various causes and symptoms but we shall concentrate here on the following points:

1. Sadness as a spiritual practise.

2. Cruelty towards oneself and towards others.

3. Ideals beyond one's capacity.

Many spiritual guides lay emphasis on the verse, *"...by a sad countenance the heart is made better." (Eccl.7:3)*.

They lay emphasis also on the words of the holy fathers mentioned in the 'Paradise of the Holy Fathers', 'Go into your cell and weep for your sins'. They even preach about tears and their benefit. All this is spiritual talk which has its benefit and its suitable time.

However, sadness can be of benefit at certain times but cannot be taken as a rule for how one should live their whole life. Such guides never talk about joy and perhaps they consider it a hindrance to repentance. They even consider laughter a sign of spiritual weakness! Those persons forget the verses of the Holy Bible, *"Rejoice in the Lord always. Again I will say, rejoice! (Phil. 4:4)* and *"But the fruit of the Spirit is love, joy, peace..." (Gal. 5:22).* The Lord Jesus Christ also says, *"... I will see you again and your heart will rejoice, and your joy no one will take from you" (Jn. 16:22).*

It is noteworthy that the Book in which is written the aforementioned verse, *"...by a sad countenance the heart is made better."* also includes the words, *"To everything there is a season... a time to weep and a time to laugh." (Eccl.3:4).*

Excessive strictness and continuous talk about sadness implant sadness in the self. Some persons may go along its path wisely and shrewdly while in other it turns into a disease! Everything in their eyes leads to sadness! Repentance calls for sadness because David the Prophet used to drench his couch with his tears every night. The ministry also calls for sadness as we see Nehemiah weeping for Jerusalem and as Jeremiah wept in his lamentations. David the Prophet also said in his Psalms, *"Indignation has taken hold of me because of the wicked, who forsake Your law."*

Humility also must be accompanied by sadness, lest joy lead one to haughtiness.!

Prayers also must be grave to a great extent! If you look at a person's features during prayers, you will find their countenance so grave and tense that you become troubled!

Truly, there is a spiritual sadness but it is accompanied by comfort and there is holy distress but accompanied by hope. So rejoicing in the Lord is mixed up with all these feelings.

On the other hand, those who lay emphasis on sadness alone without comfort, hope or rejoicing in the Lord and in His work, do not understand Christianity as they ought to nor do they understand the Bible, "the good news". They offer people a sad example.

Some people may be offended when they see people sad and sick from piety and afraid of turning into such a sad picture, always sullen, never smiling and having lost cheerfulness and the shining face! Spirituality has become to them incessant tears and continuous seriousness.

I say to those they ought to distinguish between spiritual tears which lead to joy and tears that burn and lead the soul into sullen darkness!

Is the relation with God a relation of continuous distress without any comfort? And does God the compassionate and loving want to see us only weeping and sad? Does the sadness which makes the heart better continue so after the heart is improved? Does it not give place to joy and peace?

Another point is ideals.

It is good to have ideals and we ought to do so but this may lead us to continuous sadness when we realise that we have not yet attained the desired perfection of our ideals. The path of perfection is long and going along it needs striving and patience. We ought to rejoice for every step we take along the road to reach our ideals rather than be distressed and sad for the remaining steps.

Do not think that such joy conceals pride or haughtiness of heart because it is rejoicing in God who supported us, not rejoicing in our human power and efforts.

Instead of feeling sad for what we lack, let us pray that God may help us in our weakness and perfect our deficiency.

Sadness is not a remedy; it rather may hinder us and may be used by the devil to throw us into despair.

Now we come to the spiritual remedy.

+ Spiritual remedy for sadness.

A spiritual person is completely free from the sadness that makes one sick. They may sometimes suffer sadness but it is spiritual or natural sadness for some time only. They are fortified against such extreme sadness because they have a sound spiritual basis. Here we mention seven important virtues from among other virtues which characterise such spiritual sadness; Faith in God and His work; hope; contentment and renouncing any possessions; the life of thanksgiving; joy and cheerfulness; practicality; patience and long-suffering.

We shall deal with each of these virtues briefly and mention it's relation to sadness as a remedy or protection against it.

<u>+ Faith as a remedy and a protection.</u>

We believe that God is the Almighty, who manages the universe and cares for His children. He loves them and in concerned about them; He has inscribed them on the palms of His hands (Is.49:16) and not a hair of their heads would be lost without His permission (Luke 21:18). If He does permit any tribulations to befall them, this would be for something good in the future as the Holy Bible says, "*...that all things work together for good to those who love God." (Rom. 8:28).* So, Saint James the Apostle says, *"My brethren, count it all joy when you fall into various trials" (James 1:2).*

Tribulations and temptations create in a believer joy, not distress as the Holy Bible says, *"We must through many tribulations enter the Kingdom of God." (Acts 14:22).* Through such tribulations, a believer enters into fellowship of the sufferings of the Lord Christ (Phil. 3:10) and that they fulfill the commandment to carrying the cross; *"And he who does not take his cross and follow after Me is not worthy of Me." (Matt. 10:38).* There is also the commandment of going through the narrow gate, *"Because narrow is the gate and difficult is the way which leads to life, and there are few who find it" (Matt. 7:11).*

So, a true believer does not feel sad when they face problems but on the contrary, they feel sad when they find their way void of tribulations. When they live in continuous peace, they become wary that they may have been spiritually slack or may have strayed.

A true believer rejoices in tribulations as the Apostle says, *"Therefore I take pleasure in infirmities, in reproaches, in needs, in persecution, in distresses, for Christ's sake..." (2 Cor.*

12:10)). Whenever a trouble befalls them, they feel that they are on the path of the Apostles, the fathers and the prophets who walked the before them. They rejoice in the way of Job and Lazarus the Poor because in such a way many consolations await him.

Therefore, the true believer refuses to receive their reward on earth or receive good things here in this present life. They direct all their hope towards, *"… the city which has foundations whose builder and maker is God." (Heb. 11:10).*

He endures all hardships with joy and satisfaction.

A believer needs to read about God's love, kindness and compassion and about many examples of his dealings with His children such as; His compassion on Elijah and the widow at the time of the famine (I Kings 17), His sending the angel to Daniel to close the mouths of the lions and to save the lads in the fiery furnace (Dan. 3, 6).

A believer needs to read stories about God's care for the monks and anchorites, for the martyrs and confessors and stories about God's acceptance of those who repent. Besides this faith, there must be hope in God's work for him in the future.

Here we come to another point which is hope.

+ Hope as a remedy for sadness.

By hope we mean to be optimistic about the future and not to submit to despair, however pressing the circumstances are and however bad the case may be.

A person who lives in hope is not troubled by the present tribulation but rejoices in the coming solution for it. This makes one always optimistic, trusting that any fault would be corrected and any closed door would be opened.

It is natural that despair brings forth sadness, and sadness also brings forth despair. Each is a cause for the other and a result of it but a true believer is far from both.

Through hope, he sees the solution before him, and this makes his heart happy and peaceful as the Apostle says, *"Rejoicing in hope..." (Rom.12:12).*

This joy, due to hope and assurance of a solution, makes one patient and long suffering.

+ Patience as a remedy.

Whoever wants a quick solution for their problems can easily become sad when their problem prolongs. But a patient person allows time for the problem to be solved. They are ready to wait, even for long years, trusting that the Lord will come through at the right time. They wait without being bored, sad or self-centered but have a satisfied heart completely confident in God's work.

They say, 'The Lord will certainly come and I do not care when. What concerns me is to trust that He will come.' They trust that the time which God chooses is the best and the most suitable time. It is chosen by God's wisdom and His divine dispensation. Hence the Psalmist says, *"Wait on the Lord; Be of good courage and He shall strengthen your heart; Wait, I say, on the Lord!" (Ps. 27:14).*

Would you ask, 'till when?', the Psalmist answers you, *"My soul waits for the Lord more than those who watch for the morning."* *(Ps. 130:6).* I hear you say, 'What If I cannot wait?' If I have no patience?' I tell you, let the problems teach you patience. Faith and hope also train you practically to be patient.

If you do not wait in patience, you will be tired and sad. Patience is better but let it be in confidence, trusting that God works.

Another point concerning treating sadness is contentment or renouncing possessions.

+ Contentment or renouncing possessions.

It is a virtue that removes sadness completely because a person who relinquishes any desires or lusts finds nothing to be sad about. They find no reason to be sad! So in every Mass, the words of the Bible are repeated, *"Do not love the world on the things in the world... the world is passing away, and the lust of it..." (1 Jn. 2:15,17).*

All the worldly matters are temporary, even dignity, fame, wealth and authority. If a believer loses any of these or the like, they will not be distressed or sad for it, as St. Paul the Apostle says, *"I have suffered the loss of all things, and count them as rubbish..." (Phil.3:8).*

Of course, a person who counts all things as rubbish does not become sad for losing anything. St. Augustine defines this by his famous quote, 'I sat on the top of the world, when I felt in myself that I feared nothing and desired nothing'. (Confessions of St Augustine).

If a person has not the virtue of relinquishing everything, let them acquire at least the virtue of contentment.

Let them be satisfied with what they have and require nothing more or nothing better but only what God permits them to have. Let them not think of themselves more highly than they ought to think, *"... but to think soberly, as God has dealt to each one a measure of faith." (Rom. 12:3).*

Such a person never becomes sad but says in satisfaction, 'Since the loving God is pleased with this situation for me, I am also pleased with it'. This would not only help them to get rid of sadness but would also lead them to a life of thanksgiving.

+ A life of thanksgiving as protection and a remedy.

A person who is trained to lead a life of thanksgiving never becomes sad. Hence the Apostle teaches us, *"Giving thanks always for all things..." (Eph.5:20),* and also, *"Rejoice always... in everything give thanks." (1 Thess. 5:16,18).*

So, the church arranges that every prayer begins with the thanksgiving prayer not to pray it only but to live a life of thanksgiving.

We thank God in all cases, for everything and on every occasion. Even when one of our beloved dies we begin the prayers with thanksgiving. Since we always give thanks, why then do we feel sad? Certainly there are some who recite this prayer without living it.

Train yourself then to lead a life of thanksgiving. On every occasion when something befalls you give thanks to the Lord and say to yourself, 'There must be some good behind this even though I am not aware of it. Even if there is anything evil, You will turn it into good for You are the beneficent and the lover of mankind.

A person who leads a life of thanksgiving is no doubt a true believer who believes in God's benevolence, goodness, love and wisdom. When such a believer loses thankfulness and refuses to submit to the divine will, they become sad and their faith is shaken.

On the other hand, the person who gives thanks for everything, not only rises above the level of sadness but moreover they attain the life of joy.

+ Joy as a remedy and a prevention.

A believer who rejoices in the Lord, all through their life, is never attacked by sadness. They rejoice because they have found the Lord and with Him they want nothing else nor are they sad for anything. They are content with God.

Whoever practices the life of joy, escapes sadness and its causes.

Whenever they face some trouble, they are not overly concerned by it nor go deep into its painful depths but throws it aside in order that his joy may not be disturbed. They consider sadness an attack from the devil to remove their joy and throw them into distress. They do not surrender to the attack but hold fast to the words the Lord said to His disciples, *"...your joy no one will take from you." (Jn. 16:22).*

Therefore, live a life of joy and cheerfulness and avoid the sick piety which calls you to be sad. Collect the verses which call for joy; learn them by heart and recite them every now and then and recall them whenever any troubles encompass you or whenever you are attacked by sadness.

Be sure that with joy and cheerfulness, you present a good example of sound piety and its fruit within the heart. By doing so people will be attracted to your faith, the faith that makes life happy.

On the contrary, people fear and avoid the piety which makes one's life sad because they do not want to suffer the same attacks.

By the word "joy", I do not mean the worldly joy but the joy with the Lord, which is deeper and more genuine.

By "cheerfulness" also is not meant to be dissolute and reckless as the people of the world but to be enlightened with divine joy, inner peace and faith which enlightens the face and the features, revealing that the person is happy in the holy life they lead.

A cheerful person always gives comfort to others with their cheerful countenance despite the tribulations. Whenever they are pressured by a problem, they keep it distant from their heart and do not allow it to affect them strongly. They never complicate a problem but work through in simplicity. When they face any problem, they try to solve it to the best of their ability and then they submit it wholly to God. This way they maintain their joy.

Another remedy for sadness is pragmatism.

+ Pragmatism.

By "pragmatism" we mean that a person must live in reality, not an imaginary world or with imaginary ideals. Do not put before you an imaginary life to live in or imaginary ideals you want the others to live according because when these ideals are not realised you will become sad.

If you lose a beloved, or if you miss some chance or lose something or suffer an illness, be realistic. Do whatever you ought to do and leave the rest to God. Do not live in sadness imagining an ideal position you ought to have been in.

Suppose someone is injured in an accident and as a result his leg or arm is amputated. Would they remain sad for the rest of their life? Or rather be content and conform to their new circumstances?

Another point is that you must not have your own imaginary ideals for other people, not even for the ministers of the church. Be realistic and know that they are human beings because if you discover that any of them is not. as ideal as you have imagined you will be offended or troubled and become sad. If any of them commits an error, pray for them and do not be troubled. Remember that the Holy Bible mentioned the errors of the Apostles, the Prophets and the holy people and showed how they were esteemed by God despite their errors.

Look upon the faults of-people as natural, being a part of the deviating nature of man and do not let such faults destroy you.

Many people are troubled due to the conduct of others and their errors. It seems that they consider others infallible while this is an attribute of God alone.

<u>+ Treating sadness within the scope of piety.</u>

An example of this is misunderstanding Bible verses and coming to the wrong conclusion that your sins cannot be forgiven. Such verses must be understood properly. If a person cannot reach this understanding, they have to ask those who have the appropriate Bible knowledge. If they are not convinced by someone, they have to ask another but in all this they must not fall into despair from sadness.

Some examples of such verses are the following:

1. The sin of blasphemy against the Holy Spirit. There may be someone who suffers from extreme sadness, feeling that there is no hope for them and that they will certainly perish because they fell in the sin of blasphemy against the Holy Spirit. To such a person we say:

• The persons who denied the divinity of the Holy Spirit and repented were accepted by the church.

• Blasphemy is not to have an evil thought against the Spirit or to utter a word of disdain against Him for all this may be forgiven. The only sin which has no forgiveness is that which is not followed by repentance.

• Blasphemy against the Holy Spirit is the refusal throughout one's life of the work of the Holy Spirit within your heart and so you do not repent because repentance comes through the act of the Holy Spirit.

- As there is no repentance, there will be no forgiveness but if you do repent, even after many years, your previous refusal will not be counted blasphemy because it did not continue throughout your life.

2. Another example which troubles some is the verse concerning Esau, "...*he found no place for repentance, though he sought it diligently with tears.*" *(Heb.12:17)*.

This verse applies only to the sin of selling his birthright not for any other sin he may have committed. Thus, Christ was to come of the offspring of Jacob who took the birthright for it and it was impossible that He would come of the offspring of both Jacob and Esau together. That was the matter which Esau repented for but after he had missed the opportunity.

As for any other repentance, it has forgiveness as the Lord Jesus Christ says, *"The one who comes to Me I will by no means cast out..."* *(Jn. 6:37)*. So, whenever you come to Him repenting, He will not cast you out according to His divine promise.

3. Among the faults which some fall in and which lead them to sadness is:

Concentrating on the seriousness of the sin not on God's love. In regards to this listen to what God says, *"Though your sins are like scarlet, they shall be as white as snow."* *(Is. 1:18)*.

One of the fathers also said that all the sin of mankind if compared to God's kindness and mercy, are only like a piece of mud thrown into the ocean.

So when priests and servants find someone on the verge of despair, they must not stress the awfulness of sin but on the loving kindness and compassion of God and give examples of His forgiveness to sinners.

4. Another thing which leads to sadness is: Speaking about unattainable perfection.

Besides speaking about perfection, they must speak about God who accepts any little act however trivial it may be. For example, the Lord praised the act of giving only a cup of cold water, the coming of the queen of the South to Solomon and the two mites of the poor widow. One can attain perfection gradually and God accepts every step towards it.

5. Some may fall in sadness because they try to imitate the tears of the saints.

Though the tears of repentance and love are commendable, yet we must know that the saints had cheerfulness which we can see clearly in the lives of St. Anthony, St. Serapion the Great and St. Macarius of Alexandria.

+ Lastly.

We advise all people to avoid extremes in their spiritual lives. We draw their attention to the fact that the present world is not void of troubles, so, we must be realistic and train ourselves to rejoice in spite of all tribulations.

We must not exaggerate the size of the problems or enlarge the difficulty of finding solutions for them, because every problem has a solution.

If someone becomes sad, they have to come out of it whatever the cause is. Giving in to sadness makes one troubled, ill and hinders one's spiritual life. This may even be an obstacle in the way of one's relation with the surrounding society.

Since giving in to sadness causes trouble and illness, one must not linger in it.

CHAPTER 13

LOVE OF PRAISE AND HONOUR

We have discussed in a previous article the love of outer appearances. This kind of love is a result of vain glory and includes, in particular, the love of praise and honour.

Here I like to draw your attention to an important fact, praise is one thing, and the love of praise is another. A person may be praised and commit no sin but when they begin to love this praise, they fall in error.

No doubt, superiors, distinguished persons and those who are gifted with talents are praised throughout their lives. The Apostles, the Prophets and the fathers were praised as well but did not err on hearing such praise. St. Paul the Apostle says about his ministry and that of his companions, *"By honor and dishonor, by evil report and good report..." (2 Cor.6:8).*

We see then that they were glorified and spoken well of but did not err.

The Lord Jesus Christ Himself was often praised and people were astonished at His words and teachings. People said to each other, *"We never saw anything like this...",* But He took no notice of this but only said, *"I do not receive honor from men." (Jn.5:41).*

Persons Who Do Not Like To Be Praised

1. One type hears praise as if they hear nothing, as St. Macarius the Great said, *'Do not mind honour or dishonor'.* He is dead to both.

2. A second type deplores praise which comes to them, either from people, from within themselves or from the devils.

3. A third type hates praise so exceedingly that they ascribe to themselves defects which they do not have.

An example of this is the holy monks who used to pretend to be foolish, mad or neglectful of worship. For example, the holy nun of whom St. Daniel said 'Come that I may show you the great virtues of this saint whom you call 'the foolish', St Annasimon! People of this type used to rejoice for every word of ridicule they heard. This helped them conceal their virtues and so they gained the 'great virtue' i.e., humility.

Persons Who Like To Be Praised

Those can be divided into six types according to the degree of their errors.

The first type:

Praise comes to persons of this type without any effort on their side but they feel happy and rejoice over it. Those are divided into three levels:

a) A person who enjoys hearing praise from within and nobody notices.

b) Another person hears praise and makes attempts to increase it. They direct conversations from the main subject in which they were praising them into another subject which would bring them praise also. Or they remind them of some details which they forgot so that they may praise them anew.

c) A person who likes to be praised, feels happy about it but pretends to refuse praise in such a way that makes others go on praising them. Such a person may criticize themselves so that others may speak well of them, more than at first! Here love of praise is mixed with hypocrisy.

The second type:

This is a more difficult case as the person here is not praised but they desire and love to hear praise. For this they behave in one of two ways:

a) They desire to be praised so they direct attention to subjects of their boasting or achievements. For example, they may start talking about a certain subject for which they deserve to be praised. They go on talking till they reach the point intended and then leave others to concentrate on it.

b) Or the person desires to be praised, so, they perform good works in the sight of people to be seen by them, as the Lord says in (Matt.-6:1).

The third type:

A harder case than the previous two!

Here, a person loves and desires to be praised but doesn't get it, so they seek the means that would lead others to praise them, yet they still do not get praised. This person will hate the person who does not praise them and considers them as an enemy and breaks relations with them! Though this person has done nothing to arouse their anger, yet because they did not do them courtesy with some good words or did not receive them as they had expected or with 'proper' respect they become at enmity with them!

If such a person hates those who do not praise them, how would they feel towards those who criticize them?! Certainly, such a person surrounds themselves only by those who love and admire them, by their friends and by those who give them comfort.

The fourth type:

This type includes all the previous types and goes far beyond them. A person of this type desires to be praised and is pleased to hear others praise them and they hate those who do not praise them but moreover if they do not find anyone to praise them, they praise themselves. They go on telling others about their virtuous works.

They talk much about themselves and show off every opportunity they have. They boast as though they are telling mere facts.

The fifth type:

It is a far more serious case than the previous one, for the previous one boasts of works they actually performed but this new type is a person who praises themselves for things they have not done. They may also exaggerate in praising themselves or ascribe to themselves the virtues or the works of some others.

Unlike this type of person, I remember the story of some holy monk who had excessive self-denial. When he was to perform some good work for the monastery that might earn him praise, he used to entrust a little part of the work or some part at the end to some other monk. When he was asked at the end about such work, he would dedicate all the praise to that monk who helped him and would say, "Father so and so is a blessing; he has done this and that...".

Another example of not seeking praise to oneself alone is that of the players who play as a team. Suppose that every player took the ball and kept running with it alone to shoot a goal so as to gain the glory. That team would certainly be defeated. But we see the player passes the ball to another and that passes it to someone else till the team scores a goal no matter by whom! This is self-denial which is the opposite of the love of praise.

On the other hand, a person who concentrates on themselves and neglects the role of others, ignores the work of grace with them and God's help.

Whatever good work they do, they boast about it and do not mention God's name at all. St. John the Baptist did not do this but he always drew people's attention away from himself to the Lord. The psalm also teaches us this saying, *"Not unto us, O Lord, not unto us, but to Your name give glory." (Ps.115:1).*

Certainly, any righteousness we do, is not done by us alone without divine help! For the Holy Bible says, *"Unless the Lord builds the house, they labour in vain who build it;" (Ps. 127:1).*

The success of any work does not depend only on the person who performs it but on God's help who may have arranged the help.

The sixth type:

It is the worst of all types!

It includes all the previous types and moreover, a person. of this type may love praise so exceedingly that they like to be praised alone!

They feel extremely annoyed if someone else is praised. They even get annoyed with the person who utters praise as well as the person who is praised. They envy the person praised and feel jealous; They may bad mouth the person and spite them.

Now to another point.

The Evils Resulting From The Love Of Praise

Many are the evils that result from the love of praise but we shall mention here fourteen:

1. Hypocrisy.

A person who loves praise becomes a hypocrite. They do good only to be seen by others. They do good not out of love of good itself but to show off!

2. Anger and unable to tolerate.

A person who loves praise always conceals their defects and consequently cannot endure criticism. They hate criticism and if anyone criticizes them they will not bear it. They may even become angry, enraged and provoked.

A piece of advice given or a command may trouble them since it may reveal a defect in them. They like to be right always and consider them so. Whoever reveals to them their defects will be subject to their anger.

Anger is of many kinds and it can be cured by treating the love of praise and honour! Love of praise and honour makes a person feel that any criticism or command is an insult to them. The matter may develop to be hatred.

3. Hatred.

A person who cannot accept criticism and loves praise does not only hate those who criticize them but also those who do not praise them. They may also hate those who praise someone else, especially if the praise is for something they took part in. They want to have all honour themselves!

4. Envy.

A person who loves praise and honour, envies others who are given praise and honour. They do not like anyone to be better than them!

5. Condemning and defaming others.

A person who likes to be superior to others criticizes and condemns them. They will attack their personality or work in order to appear better than them.

6. They are hard to love.

People hate boasting and those who act aloof so a person behaving this way loses the esteem of others and because they are critical of others, they lose people's love also.

7. A person who loves praise loves also the best positions.

They love grandeur, love showing off and loves to be the first to gain the interest of people. They love to be the subject of others talk. This makes them enter into arguments and quarrels with others and if they find anyone superior to them, they try to ridicule and mock them!

8. It could also be a cause for them to lie.

They are willing to lie if it brings them praise. They may falsely ascribe to themselves certain virtues. They may convince others of an ideal picture of themselves which they do not really have. They may lie about others to defame them or bring them down in the sight of others so they appear better.

9. They may plot and spread rumours or gossips.

They plot against whomever they may think of as their rivals in honour. Their purpose is to stop them from receiving the praise or honour they believe they deserve.

10. They may be filled with evil.

They may desire the death of someone else in order to take their place! They may desire the failure and loss of others in order to occupy their positions. They may wish that some colleague would be exposed to the anger of their superiors or be accused of some offence so that they may shine and have no rivals.

They might not fabricate accusations against others, but they feel inner pleasure if such accusations are raised by others!

11. A person who loves praise is often a troublemaker in their social environment.

They are always a burden to people around them and their conduct leads others to condemn them or to avoid dealing with them. Their attempts to be continuously in the spotlight and to have all praise makes them unable to give others any opportunity.

They also do not accept any advice or counsel. They become a problem which no one can solve.

They may be upset and fuming without any logical reason.

They can be ill with any illness but refuse council regarding his illness or refuses any remedy and does not feel that he is ill.

They are easily affected and ready to grumble.

They cannot endure anyone and nobody can endure them. If some visitor came and greeted someone else more warmly than they, they would be annoyed!

12. A person who loves praise may become changeable and unpredictable.

They do not take a clear path but walk in any path that may gain them praise. They change according to whatever image people present.

With the respectable they are respectable and wise and with the merry, they are witty to the utmost. With those who like to be silent, they keep silent and with those who like to talk, they talk to show their vast knowledge.

If they find that their defense of someone would bring them praise, they defend them.

If they gain honour by speaking ill of someone, they speak ill of them and exaggerate in doing so!

They defend the truth if this will make them a hero but if it causes them harm or makes others condemn them, they say to themselves, *"Therefore the prudent keep silent at that time, for it is an evil time." (Amos.5:13).*

They want to be praised by whatever the means, even though the means may contradict each other!

If they find someone who leads an ascetic life, they refrain from eating in front of them. If they find someone who enjoys eating, they offer them many sorts of food at the table.

They change their character or personality according to the person they are dealing with. Their purpose is to gain peoples approval, confidence and praise and to be in a dignified position before them!

13. A person who loves praise may become proud and arrogant.

For a person to become proud is not good and can lead to many bad results. However, if they find that they can gain the same honour through humility, they would not hesitate to appear humble!

14. A person who loves praise loses their spiritual life completely and loses both heaven and earth.

They lose their spiritual life, partly because of the said faults and partly because any virtues they practice loses its spirituality because their aim became the love of praise. This makes them no longer virtues.

Whatever they do and however they strive, they would stand before God empty-handed and would have no reward from Him because they would have taken their reward on earth. They sell all their good deeds for pride and vain glory, for praise and dignity. They deserve to hear the words of Father Abraham, *"...in your lifetime you received your good things..." (Luke 16:.25)*. They practiced no virtue at all for God's sake. Thus they lose their eternity, they don't gain the earth and lose honour also.

They lose eternity due to the sins which they fall in. They lose people's love and respect and lives miserably on earth; they seek praise by any means, they compete with others and envy them and lose their inner peace.

They lose honour as well according to the true words of St. Isaac, *'Honour escapes from whoever seeks it, and seeks whoever escapes from it cunningly.'*

The Remedy For The Love Of Praise And Honour

We shall give you here some pieces of advice and some practices for you to choose what suits you most; because as the causes and signs of the love of praise differ from one person to another, so what pieces of advice fit others may not fit you.

The first piece of advice is:

1. Vanity of the worldly honour.

You ought to know well that people's praise does not lead you to the Kingdom of God. It may rather hinder you from attaining it.

You will not enter the Kingdom according to the judgment of people but according to God's pleasure.

Very false indeed is the praise of people. Some may praise you out of courtesy and some others to encourage you or to be polite. Some may praise you for a certain purpose they have or to flatter you or merely to please you knowing that you like such praise!!

Do not be deceived by this praise nor believe whatever is said. Do not be pleased with it either, whether it is right or false.

Do not let praise create within you a kind of vain glory for this is dangerous for your eternity. Rather say with the Lord Jesus, *"I do not receive honour from men." (Jn. 5:41).*

Even though you had done good deeds, say to yourself, 'What

benefit do I receive if I take the reward of all my labour here on this transient earth, whether that be praise or dignity, positions or authority. In eternal life I shall hear the fearful words,

"...remember that in your lifetime you received your good things." (Luke 16:25).

Therefore I shall have no portion up there in heaven! Indeed how dangerous it is, to sell eternal life and buy this world!!

2. Any praise is temporary.

Who praises you today, may not praise you tomorrow and may speak ill of you the day after tomorrow! People are not stable in their praise and may not be telling the truth. Even if they were true they may be praising a certain situation which may change.

Some people may praise you to your face but speak ill behind your back. You may not hear their criticism but others may hear it.

Those who honour you for your position or for your prestige or authority, may be giving honour to such a position not to you. If you lose such a position by leaving it or being removed from it, they will not honour you as they did before!

There may be some people who praise you much and honour you greatly but do not continue to do so. They may change due to the opinions of others. Some may envy you for what you attained or become your enemies for some reason and they may spread rumours concerning you which would change others opinion towards you! Many lies and falsehoods may be spread by people which leads others to think less of you and treat you differently!

Hence, as you were praised undeservedly before, you suffer now undeserved oppression!!

So, let your main concern be to please God and to obtain the heavenly reward. Do not concentrate on the honour which people give you, for it may be false or temporary!

3. Getting rid of· self-admiration.

The most dangerous praise which fights a person is praising themselves. Listen to what the Bible says; *"Do not be wise in your own eyes."(Prov.3:7).* It says also, *"The rich man is wise in his own eyes." (Prov. 28:11),*

Since it is wrong to be wise in one's own eyes, it is even more wrong that a person be *"...righteous in his own eyes." (Job 32:1).*

Such inner pride has its disadvantages and many sins result from it. Besides arrogance and vain glory there are other disadvantages:

+ You may despise the wisdom of others and speak to them haughtily!

+ You will not accept criticism or advice. You will clash with whomever contradicts you and you will attack them. You will lose objectivity of thinking and make any difference of opinions a personal matter considering that any objection to your views is an objection to your person!

+ You will not seek the wisdom that comes from God nor the wisdom of others!

+ You may reach a state of self-satisfaction and stop developing. Beautiful indeed are the words of our Lord Jesus Christ addressed to the Father, *"I thank You, Father. because You have hidden these things from the wise and prudent, and have revealed them to babes."* *(Matt. 11:25).*

Stand then before God admitting your ignorance in order to take wisdom from Him and do not despise the wisdom of any person lest God should deprive you of wisdom.

Try always to benefit from everyone, for the Holy Bible teaches us to learn even from the ant (Prov. 7:6) and from the lilies of the field (Matt. 6:38).

Whatever level you attain in wisdom and knowledge, remember the words of the Holy Bible; *"... lean not on your own understanding; ..."* *(Prov. 3:5).*

As for the person who is righteous in their own eyes, they are people who have not yet known the truth about themselves, nor do they know the measures of righteousness!

In order that such a person may cure themselves and get rid of this self-righteousness and self-admiration, they have to follow this piece of advice:

4. Remember your sins.

Whenever you are praised by people or by yourself, remember your sins and remember your shortcomings, your falls and your defects. Say to yourself in complete frankness; 'People praise me because they do not know me. If ever they knew some of my shortcomings, they would change the way the treat me!

Say also, 'Thank you God because you have protected me. I cannot accept the praise of others but rather I should acknowledge Your protecting and blessing me! Should I forget my sins and begin to praise myself as if I do not know myself and my defects!'

If the remembrance of your sins does not prevail over praise, it will at least diminish its effect on you. It will create an equilibrium within you and keep you from falling prey to the love of praise. It will make you alert to your true self and limit your self- admiration.

If you do not remember your previous sins, at least be afraid of falling in any sins afterwards for the Holy Bible says, *"Pride goes before destruction, and a haughty spirit before a fall." (Prov. 16:18)*.

If you find yourself content or pleased with praise, say to yourself, 'I am now liable to fall. I have already fallen through this praise. It is better for me to think humbly. If I am fought with righteousness, I shall remember my sins and if I am fought with wisdom and knowledge, I shall not forget what knowledge I lack and what sins I have fallen in through my thoughts.

Another remedy is:

5. Remember that there are people spiritually better than you.

Whenever you are fought with the thought that you possess certain virtues or knowledge remember that you are nothing.

Compare yourself to those who have attained higher levels.

Thanks God that He has provided us with saints who have excelled in virtues so that when we compare ourselves to them, we are humbled.

Regarding knowledge also, our fathers and some of our contemporaries have attained higher levels than ours.

So compare yourself to those who have attained higher spiritual and virtuous levels than yourself to be humble and do not compare yourself to those who are weaker than yourself.

Even in this case you may be fought with another matter. You may say, 'Indeed I am weak and of a lesser level than that of the saints and the holy but I feel myself of a higher level than those surrounding me.' How should you answer these thoughts? I tell you that even those whom you criticize may possess certain virtues and qualities that you lack. That was the lesson which the Lord Jesus Christ taught the Pharisees!

The Pharisee who saw himself better than the tax-collector and said to God, *"God, I thank You that I am not like other men, extortioners, unjust, adulterers, or even as this tax collector…"* *(Luke 18:11)*. This Pharisee was shown by the Lord Jesus that in spite of his fasting and giving the tithes was surpassed by the tax-collector who was humble and broken hearted.

The Lord also proved to Simeon the Pharisee, who received Him in his home, that the sinner woman washed His feet with her tears was better than him. She surpassed that Pharisee in love, generosity and humility (Luke 7:44-47).

So, if you compare yourself to someone else and think you are better than them in certain aspects, search for the points which perhaps they surpass you in.

Do not say 'I am better than such a person in knowledge; but say he is better than me in simplicity and purity of heart'! Do not say 'I surpass him in fasting and prayers; but say he surpasses me in long-suffering and tolerance'!

Be sure that if you forsake your pride, you will find that most people possess virtues which you lack.

St. Ephraim the Syrian found in the flamboyant woman, who was a sinner, a virtue which he lacked! St. Anthony also heard the voice of God in the woman who took off her clothes before him to take a bath! St. Macarius took a lesson from the shepherd and benefited from it. St. Moses the Black saw in the lad Zechariah, the gift of the Holy Spirit, which he was in need of.

God often chooses the small to rebuke the great!!

He chose the heathen captain of ship to rebuke Jonah the great prophet (Jon 1:6). God also chose the Canaanite woman to condemn the faith of her generation as a whole. He chose Lazarus the poor to rebuke the rich man. He chose the foolish things of the world to put to shame the wise, and chose the weak things of the world, the base, the despised and the things which are not to bring to nothing the things that are. (1 Cor. 1:27,28).

So, do not think of yourself highly lest you should have to say 'Ye, the high tower, how did you fall'?

If you think yourself great and powerful, remember that the devil takes great pleasure in making the great and the powerful fall. The devil fights them very hard and with great violence. The Holy Bible says about sin, *"She has cast down many wounded, and all who were slain by her were strong men." (Prov. 7:26).*

However, if you see yourself righteous in spite of all this and you fear not to fall, let me give you this piece of advice also.

6. Remember the work of grace with you.

You are stable and did not fall till now, not because you are strong but because grace supports you. So do not boast vainly of your power because if grace forsakes you, you will be like the others who fall! Listen to the Psalm which says, *"Unless the Lord guards the city, the watchman stays awake in vain." (Ps.127:1).*

If you find that you have escaped the attacks of the devil, praise the Lord for His help and say, *"If it had not been the Lord who was on our side... then they would have swallowed us alive when their wrath was kindled against us." (Ps.124:2,3).*

You are just an instrument in God's hand with which He does something good. So why do you concentrate on the instrument and forget the hand that works with it! Why do you forget the work of grace within you and ascribe God's act to yourself?

Say to yourself always, 'I am nothing but a handful of dust and ashes, or a totally weak human! If grace forsakes me, I become nothing at all. Let me remember the words of the Lord Jesus Christ, *"...without Me you can do nothing." (Jn.15:5).*

You should acknowledge this fact by saying, 'If grace forsakes me because of my pride, then I shall fall and be revealed as the weak person I am'.

If you continue to take credit and accept pride in the work of Gods' grace in you, God may leave you to work by yourself. If this happens, you will certainly fall because without Him you can do nothing (Jn. 15:5).

So if you want grace to continue to work with you, do not praise yourself nor accept the praise of others.

I do not mean by not accepting praise, that you refuse to hear it, for you may not be able to do that. Also if you do refuse, people may praise you more and so the opposite happens. But what I mean is that you must not let praise enter into your heart, must not be pleased with it, believe it or be delighted with it.

Another piece of advice.

7. Endure the criticism of others.

Some try to escape from praise and for that purpose they may criticise themselves before others. This may bring them more praise whether they desired it or not. So, when St. Serapion the Great found a young monk who could not bear to be given advice and whose face grew red, he said to him, ''Do not blame yourself falsely. It is not humility to criticise yourself but real humility is to endure and accept the criticism from others.'

How easy it is for a person to say, 'I am a sinner and a weak person' but at the same time cannot endure to hear these words from others. Do they criticise themselves falsely? Or do they do it to be considered as humble? If so they are in fact a hypocrite!!

Or do they say about themselves that they are a sinner because their self-criticism does not hurt them while the criticism of others hurts them!

A person who is really humble accepts criticism and considers that they may be reminded of their sins through others. They may accept it in return for a previous praise they received, or to conceal their virtues. They may accept it as an earthly punishment for their previous sins, whether such sins were known or not.

Accepting criticism from others gladly is considered by the fathers the other cheek turned to people.

St. Anthony said, 'Whenever you are criticised by someone, you have to blame yourself within, in order to make an equilibrium between your interior and your exterior'.

Thus, two matters will be achieved; you will not be troubled within, nor will you return the insult to the other outside.

A person who loves praise and honour cannot endure insults and may respond to an insult in various ways:

a) The simplest way is to respond to an insult by defending oneself and proving one's innocence. However, defending oneself whether it is right or wrong depends upon the motives, if they are pure or not.

b) A person may respond to an insult with a similar insult or one which is more severe. In such a case, a person will have avenged themselves and will have broken the commandment of the Lord which says, "...*resist not an evil person...*" *(Matt. 5:39),* and the commandment which says, *"Beloved, do not avenge yourselves.." (Rom.12:19).* Such a person will also have gone astray from the love which is said to, *"...bears all things..."* and *"...does not seek its own." (1 Cor. 13:7,5).*

c) A person may also respond to an insult by complaining and defaming others in order to gain their sympathy and convince them that they are oppressed. They appear as a victim in order to make others avenge them! In such a way, they will have taken revenge and also fallen in many other sins. Another point is that a person who always thinks that they are oppressed can never improve as a person because they always justify themselves.

d) They may respond to an insult within their heart. They may consider the person who insults them as an enemy and treat them as such. They may quarrel with them or simply severe their relations with them. This would be their positive response to what they consider is an insult. All this is due to their love of honour!

On the other hand, a person who cares not for worldly honour is not concerned about all this nor do they take an unfriendly attitude towards it. A humble person does not consider every criticism an insult. They take the criticism as an opportunity to better themselves and may thank the criticizer for revealing a defect which needed remedy. Thus, they do not become an enemy to whoever criticizes or rejects them or who disapproves of some defect in their behaviour. They would rather examine themselves with all love and humility to find if they really have such a defect. In such a case the person who guided them to it will have helped them to attain salvation and overcome their defects.

In regard to accepting criticism, St. John Chrysostom said, 'Take as a friend the person who speaks ill of you'.

8. Concealing one's virtues.

A person who does not love praise, conceals their virtues from people in order not to be praised. They do good in secret and with good intention, according to the Lord's commandment (Matt.6).

Indeed, if you do good for God's sake not for people, then why would you be concerned if people see it or not?

Here I remember a story which happened with Anba Bemwa. One day St. Melania, before being a nun, came to him with a great amount of gold for she was wealthy. She asked him to spend it on the needs of the monks in the inner wilderness. The saint called his disciple and gave him the bag of money without opening it and asked him to distribute the money among the needy monks in the wilderness. St. Melania said to the saint, 'But father, you did not open it to know the amount?' Here the saint looked at her deeply and said, 'Daughter, since you offer this money to God, He certainly knows its amount!' St. Melania took a spiritual lesson regarding vain glory when alms giving.

Let us remember here the words of the Lord, *"When you do a charitable deed, do not let your left hand know what your right hand is doing." (Matt.6:3).* What does this divine commandment mean? How profound is it! It means that it is not enough that people don't know the good deeds you do but you should not let yourself know your own virtues, conceal them from yourself. Do not mention them, remember them or think of them.

Some people offer to the poor without counting what they give in order not to know. Thus they carry out the commandment literally. Some others give and try not to remember what they gave exactly nor add up at the end of each period the total sum of what they gave.

God does not count what He gave you, so, do not count what you give Him.

Forget whatever good you have done and remember it no more. Do not mention it before people nor think of it within you. Do not intend for people to see what you give or what you do or to make them praise you for what you do.

This does not mean that you stop from doing good so that people should not see you. Then you will be considered negligent regarding your spiritual life. But do good for goodness sake out of love for those whom you do good to and out of love for God who gave you the ability to do good. Do not mind whether people see you or not.

Sometimes, being seen by people urges one to do good but it is not a spiritual urge but only the urge to gain praise

Here we remember the story of a Syrian monk who dwelt in the desert of Scetis. One day he came to St. Macarius the Great saying, 'Father, while I was in my country I used to spend the days fasting but here in the wilderness I feel very hungry before sunset. Why is this?'. St. Macarius answered him, 'When you were in your country, people saw you and so in your fast you fed on vain glory but here, in the wilderness, where no one sees you, you feel hungry!'

In concealing virtues, a believer may be fought by the desire to be an example but a humble person does not consider themselves an example because they find nothing in themselves which deserves to be followed.

A humble person addresses God in their prayer saying, 'O Lord, You know my life, how sinful it is. You have protected me and did not wish to expose me before people. Should I then make use of this protection and go as far as to make of myself an example! Who am I to be an example!'

So we shouldn't make our aim to be an example even though we might become one without our will according to God's dispensation. A person who aims to be an example falls easily in pride and hypocrisy. They mislead people by concealing their faults and revealing only their virtues!

A humble person who escapes from being an example, may reveal to people his defects and weak points. Some monks of the desert came to Mother Sarah and told her about their weaknesses. She said to them, 'Truly you are of the Scetis (the desert) because you conceal your virtues and ascribe to yourselves vices which you do not have.

St. Bishoy used to leave any spiritual practice if it was revealed. He would then adopt another practice that no one knew. This does not mean that you ought to leave any good practice you follow, for this may be harmful for you. Rather be firm in every good practice for your spiritual improvement rather than for the sake of being seen by people. Even when you conceal your virtues, do it wisely.

However, we say that some people, due to their positions, ought to be examples lest others should be offended by them, such as priests, leaders and those who are responsible for others. They must be examples by their nature not falsely and out of hypocrisy. They may have many hidden virtues but they must have no offensive sins. They must not think much of their known virtuous life. They concentrate mainly on their spiritual growth and say with the Apostle, "...*forgetting those things which are behind and reaching forward to those things which are ahead.*" *(Phil.3:13).* Among the important means of escaping from the love of praise and honour is the next point.

10. Having no desire for authority.

Having authority is not in itself a sin, for God set ranks even among the angels. A person who is a leader and holding a great position can be meek and humble in spite of it. The fault is not in the position but in the love of that position.

A person who seeks high positions, desires glories pertaining to the love of the world not to the spiritual life. Such a person is spoiled and becomes exalted in heart if they attain the high position. They may think that they have become of great worth and expect people to treat them so.

Those that long for presidency are quick to fall into daydreaming!!

They may daydream that they have become someone important and that they were received with praise, esteem and respect. They imagine that they can achieve great works which no one else has ever achieved! All this imagery is due to vain glory. God may permit that certain responsibilities be entrusted to such a day-dreamer. Yet they eventually fail because one can imagine oneself doing things which in fact one is not able to do.

An example of this is the story of an old father who went to visit a monk who was fought with vain glory. That monk was, at the time of the visit, imagining himself delivering a sermon. He was preaching in a loud voice which the old father could hear outside. At the end of the imaginary sermon, the monk blessed the people and let them go in peace. At this point the old father knocked at the door and the young monk opened, not knowing if he heard him or not and what he would say. So he said to the old father, 'I am sorry, father, I fear you have been waiting for a long time at the door'. The old father smiling said, 'Son, I came when you were dismissing the people!'

Beware then of daydreams and avoid imagining things which you do not possess.

St. John of Assiut was asked one day, 'Is it proper for a person to require a rank or an authority in order to be able to reform the deviants and put an end to wickedness?' The saint answered, 'No because if such a person longs to have authority, what would they do when they actually attain the authority? If they are not humble and have faults what sort of authority would they be? If such a person is puffed up though holding no position, what would they be like when they gain the high position?'

The high positions may be of no harm to those who are spiritually mature because they are humble but it is harmful to the immature.

St. Orosius, a successor of St. Pachomius the Great said, 'The presidency is harmful to those persons who have not yet become mature'. He gave an example of this saying, 'If you take an unburnt brick and throw it into water, it will dissolve. But if the brick is burnt, it will survive water and even become harder. So it is with the person who holds authority before attaining maturity, that is, before being burnt with fire, I mean with the experience of the world. Such a person is liable to perish because they are not yet free of vain glory'.

People who work under the authority of someone who loves vain glory are to be pitied. That person in authority destroys themselves and others for the sake of the glory which they seek. So it is very dangerous to ordain as a priest a persons who loves worldly dignity.

If you are not humble of hearted, do not seek priesthood. Desire to be a sheep of the flock tended by others rather than to be responsible for a flock. Since you are not able to win yourself, how would you win many souls for the Lord? When you had no burdens, you could not help your salvation, how then would you be able to save a great many people from the evil of the world!

A humble person who seeks their own salvation, feels within themselves unable to help others and hence escapes from the priesthood. However, if God calls you and makes of you a priest, ask Him to give you power to and to support you. If you are given a position to satisfy a need of the church, do not trust your power and your talents but pour yourself before God that He may work with you, in you and through you. Be only an instrument which He would use according to the depth of the riches of His wisdom.

If you become a priest or if you hold a position, be humble of heart. Do not think that you have become a pillar of the church and do not behave in arrogance. Consider yourself just a servant and behave like one. Consider that the Lord Jesus Christ washed the feet of His disciples. He said of Himself, *"For even the Son of man did not come to be served, but to serve, and to give His life a ransom for many." (Mark 10:45).*

One day, a newly ordained priest asked me to give him advice for the ministry. I said to him, *"Be a son amidst your brothers, and a brother amidst your sons".*

This means that he should never exalt himself and thus remains always humble. If he wants to enjoy the dignity of his position, he will destroy himself. Positions are not means of gaining dignity, glory or honour for oneself but are for the ministry. Whoever behaves as a minister (a servant) while holding such positions will be elevated by God. St. Barsinofious said, 'Do not think highly of yourself regarding any matter and let not others think highly of you and you will be comfortable'. That is because people love those who are humble and dislike those who love praise or honour.

Those who loves positions may also clash with others who have the same desire and who may be superior to them as rivals. But those who love the lowest place will have no rivals.

If you gain a position of authority do not misuse it but treat all gently. Be sure to know that you have such authority for work responsibilities not to misuse or abuse when dealing with other. Give those you have authority over every respect and love. Know that you and your subjects are equal before God. Perhaps some of them even have a greater rank in the sight of God. Feel within you that you are their colleague, though you are their senior and deal with them with simplicity and love.

A person who uses authority to exalt themselves, deviates from its objective and from the humility required for it. The same may be said with respect to the father and husband in the family, the teacher towards their pupils, the guide towards those they guide and with respect to everyone who holds a position of leadership, fatherhood or pastorship.

St. Pachomius used to refuse to let his sons carry his luggage for him. He liked to be like them in every service as St. Paul the Apostle taught, *"...these hands have provided for my necessities, and for those who were with me." (Acts 20:34).*

Thus, the fathers were models to their sons in the ministry and in humility. In this way they gained their love and their submission as well. They never considered themselves heads but fathers, not holding an authority but having great hearts full of kindness and compassion.

St. Sisoes was entrusted with a new brother to teach but he never gave him an order. So the fathers blamed him for not teaching the brother but he answered, 'I am not a master to give orders. If he wants to learn he can see how I work and do as I do.'

So, humility of the heart is a basic condition for anyone who may hold a leading position lest they should destroy themselves and those under their leadership. Also they must not be a bad example in their leadership. They have to lead others with love, teaching and by a good example; not by wielding authority, giving orders and punishments.

As for the humble who flee from authority, I give them the example of St. Pinovius.

St. Pinovius

His story reached us from John Cassian (who established monasticism in France).

St. Pinovius presided over a monastery of more than two hundred monks in the area of Borollos. He was very humble and venerated. He was highly esteemed by many who loved his holiness, his virtuous love and his spiritual talents. They revered him also for his old age and priesthood. One day he addressed himself saying, 'What is the end of this veneration which I receive everyday? I fear I am receiving my reward here on earth. Where is then the narrow gate and the difficult way which the Holy Bible teaches saying, *"...we must through many tribulations enter the Kingdom of God." (Acts 14:22)*. He then escaped from the monastery disguised as a layman and went south till be reached one of the monasteries of St. Pachomius the great in Esna. He knocked at the door asking to be accepted into the monastery. They were astonished and inquired, 'Who was that old man who came to be a monk! Was he coming after being satisfied with the world and its enjoyment!' So, they dismissed him saying, 'You are not accepted'. He persisted and they said, 'You will not be able to endure the hardships of monasticism'. He again insisted and stood at the door for some time not eating or drinking anything. When they saw his long-suffering and patience, they accepted him in the monastery on condition that he would remain a layman and not be ordained as a monk!

After being accepted into the monastery they told him to assist a young monk to look after the garden of the monastery. He did not object and obeyed the young monk who gave him orders as to a servant. The saint was pleased as this is what he longed for!

The young monk treated him harshly and the saint was strictly obedient. In the middle of the night, while the monks were asleep, he used to do the work which the others found disgusting, such as cleaning the toilets. The monks were not aware who did that work. He continued in that service for three years. He used to say to the Lord, 'Thank you my Lord for your gifts, for you gave me what I desired. Here there is no respect nor veneration but only orders and obedience'

Then, one day a monk from the monasteries of Borollos came to visit the monastery where the saint was. He saw St. Pinovius carrying manure to put around the trees but he doubted and could not believe his eyes. He heard him reciting his psalms in his known voice, so he was sure and knelt before him. This was made known to all and he was taken in great honour to his own monastery….but he escaped again to Bethlehem. There he worked as a servant in the cell of John Cassian. There also another monk came to visit the place and met the saint. He recognised him and took him again in great respect to his monastery. When John Cassian came to Egypt, he visited the saint and wrote about him in his books. St. Pinovius is a living example of- fleeing from authority and honour.

We put such examples from the monastic life before us as mere models of fleeing from the love of positions of authority or from honour but some may not be able to imitate them as they are living in the world. They are just lessons from which we learn at least to avoid and fly from the desire for honour. If God wills to put us in a position of authority, we must behave humbly. We should do the work of a leader but with love, not as being a chief.

CHAPTER 14

VIOLENCE

Violence Is A Compound Sin

Christianity does not approve of violence in whatever form because it is not a spiritual conduct that includes a number of sins:

1. It is a compound sin and a detested sin.

Violence is hated by all people and whoever behaves violently cannot gain the favour of any person. We shall try to analyse violence to reveal what sins are included in it.

2. Violence demonstrates a cruel heart.

A person with a tender heart cannot be violent but behaves gently, their words are also gentle and well-selected, they do not allow themselves to hurt anyone's feelings.

3. Violence is the opposite of meekness.

Those who behave violently lose their meekness immediately. So, Christianity called for meekness as well as for gentleness and calmness.

In the Sermon on the Mount, the Lord Jesus Christ put meekness at the beginning of the Beatitudes. He said, *"Blessed are the meek, for they shall inherit the earth." (Matt.5:5).*

When He called us to imitate Him who is perfect in all attributes and virtues, He said, *"Learn from Me, for I am gentle and lowly in heart..." (Matt.11:29).*

Jesus was meek and never used violence. It was said of Him in the Holy Bible, *"....A bruised reed He will not break, and smoking flax he will not quench." (Matt. 12:20).*

4. Violence is not compatible with love.

Christianity teaches us that love, meekness and gentleness are the fruit of the Holy Spirit (Gal. 5:22). It said, *"God is love, and he who abides in love abides in God, and God in him." (1Jn. 4:16).*

A spiritual person treats their problems with love not with violence, because through love they win God and people. If they behave with violence, they will lose all.

5. Violence is also an aggressive sin.

Christianity disproves of aggression and it is said, *"Do not be overcome by evil, but overcome evil with good, (Rom.12:21),* and also, *"Bless those who persecute you, bless and do not curse. Repay no one evil for evil... If it is possible, as much as depends on you, live peaceably with all men... do not avenge yourselves... Therefore if your enemy hungers, feed him; if he thirsts, give him a drink..." (Rom. 12:14-20).*

Christianity which disapproves of anger, cannot allow violence or aggression.

The Apostle says, *"...let every man be swift to hear, slow to speak, slow to wrath, for the wrath of man does not produce the righteousness of God." (James 1:19,20).* The Holy Bible says also, *"Let all bitterness, wrath, anger... be put away from you..."* *(Eph. 4:31),* and *"Make no friendship with an angry man, and with a furious man do not go..." (Prov. 22:24).*

Christianity is against human anger because it is the first step to aggression, violence and murder.

The Lord Jesus Christ says in the Sermon on the Mount, *"...whoever is angry with his brother without a cause shall be in danger of the judgment." (Matt. 5:22)*. Here we distinguished between anger without a cause and from holy anger, which is for God's sake and conducted in a spiritual manner that is far from the body and its inflamed nerves.

6. Violence demonstrates hatred.

Anger develops into hatred and hatred in turn into aggression, violence and a desire to do harm to others. Hence the Holy Bible says, *"Whoever hates his brother is a murderer." (1 Jn. 3:15:)*. Even though there is no physical murder, there is a murder through intention or thought which are all branches of one sin.

7. Violence hides a desire for revenge or at least shows intolerance.

Violence is the condition of a person who cannot endure, so they want to avenge themselves and regain their right or what they consider as their right. They do not leave the matter in the hands of God who said, *"...vengeance is Mine, I will repay..." (Rom. 12:19)*. Nor do they leave the matter to the law or to society.

Christianity does not call only for long - suffering because long-suffering is a negative virtue but it calls for love which is a positive virtue.

Love and violence do not go together because the Holy Bible

says, *"Love suffers long and is kind... bears all things, ... does not seek its own." (1 Cor. 13:4-7).*

In the case of violence, love vanishes and another thing appears instead, which is the ego or the self.

8. The 'self' appears at the time of violence.

A person uses violence as self-assertion or self-defense. At the same time, they want others to submit to them.

Christianity powerfully and clearly fights the self as the Lord Jesus Christ says expressly, *"If anyone desires to come after Me, let him deny himself..." (Matt. 16:24).* In fact, violence does not achieve self-assertion but rather demonstrates weakness! How is this explained?

9. During violence, one has no control over oneself.

A calm person restrains themselves but a violent person loses self-restraint and cannot control their nerves or their wrath. They may behave rashly in a way that shows that they cannot control even their mind or their thoughts. The Holy Bible says, *"He who rules his spirit is better than he who takes a city." (Prov.16:32).*

10. Violence is proof of weakness.

Violence Demonstrates Weakness

If a person's heart is not full of love and their mind cannot solve problems wisely and calmly and if they cannot control their nerves prudently, then they resort to violence. Here violence demonstrates helplessness and inability to behave properly. It is a fact that most violent people are weak. They have weak nerves and are incapable of long-suffering or sensible thinking. I shall give you here some examples:

A teacher who treats their pupils violently is weak. They cannot keep discipline among their students and so bursts out in anger, beats this pupil, dismisses that, insults and punishes others. They surely are weak because if they were strong, they would not behave in such a manner. They would be able to control the class with their strong personality, their intelligence or attractive explanation, their mirth and gentleness or because of the love of the pupils for them. But this teacher lacking all such good attributes resorts to violence out of helplessness.

Another example is the mother who beats her children.

A mother who cannot control her child resorts to violence. She beats them, insults, threatens or frightens them in any way!! That is because she does not have the experience or the knowledge of the educational means of treating children. If she had such knowledge, she would win her child without violence. Violence here is a means to conceal inability or a mere sign of helplessness.

It may also be a means to conceal an inner weakness, which is perhaps a lack of endurance. An intelligent person can overcome their problems easily, wisely and prudently.

Hence, the Apostle says, *"We then who are strong ought to bear with the scruples of the weak and not to please ourselves..."* *(Rom. 15:1).*

Kinds Of Violence

1. Hurtful violence.

This kind of violence includes beating, murder and all physical or psychological torment such as frightening and startling others. All this is considered nervous violence.

2. Another kind of violence is intimidation.

This kind includes the crimes of kidnapping persons and high jacking planes and ships, blasting cars and using explosives, demolishing, destroying things and arousing terror. All these are awful crimes.

3. Wars also are a kind of violence.

Wars have been known since ancient times. They are aspects of violence especially when they are aggressive not defensive. However, there are wars which demonstrate a deeper violence i.e., nuclear wars or the wars which use poisonous gases, murderous and burning weapons. Also on the same level are the wars which destroy whole cities, annihilate civilizations and leave behind many deformed and retarded.

4. Violence on a personal level such as destroying one's spirits.

Some examples of this kind of violence are harsh reproach, cruel rebuke, concentrating on someone's faults continuously and destroying one's personality. Another aspect of violence may be insults.

5. Violent insults.

This includes bitter sneering, disdain, defaming, abusing, slander, disregard, breaking relations, insulting, reviling and other kinds of moral and mental murder. All this may be accompanied by threatening words.

Another aspect of violence is reproach.

6. Violent reproach.

It includes harsh cruel blame which hurts and which may be over a trivial matter. Such blame may continue long or be in front of others. It may be accompanied by nervous behaviour. It may become a person's nature so that they blame others for everything whether serious or trivial until they lose their friends.

Some poet said in this regard; *'If you blame your friend for everything, you will eventually find no one to blame. Live then alone or be on good terms with your brother, for he may be guilty at one time and innocent at another. If you do not drink bitter water with dust you will be thirsty, for no one drinks clear water always'.*

There is another different kind of violence which is negative violence.

7. Negative violence.

A person who is not able to-show positive violence may resort to negative violence. This could be continuous sadness, continuous weeping, refraining from eating, sad silence, withdrawal etc.! All these are kinds of silent, calm violence but they still hurt others.

There may be another kind of violence which is not directed towards others but works within, that is lusts.

8. Violent lusts.

There may be certain lusts which fight a person violently until they are completely destroyed. Some examples of these lusts are; greed, narcotics and pride. It is known that lusts never calm down till they are satisfied.

Lusts may be accompanied by destructive thoughts which cannot be overcome till the person is destroyed. They are so serious that some people treat them with medication to be relieved.

The Causes Of Violence

1. Among these causes is a cruel nature.

Some people are cruel by nature and they always deal with others with cruelty. If this cruelty increases, it will turn into violence.

Cruelty may be due to certain social circumstances which encompass a person and which may come to them through inheritance.

2. Nervousness that could be a result of weariness or overwork or being overloaded with responsibilities. In this case the person is not able to endure the pressure they are under and so responds violently.

3. Violence may be due to helplessness or with the purpose of concealing one's weakness as we have mentioned before.

4. Violence may be due also to a nervous disorder or a mental disease.

The Italian psychological school came up with this theory. They say that every criminal is sick and we should search for the disease that led them to commit their crime. It is well known also that some mental and nervous diseases are accompanied by violence. However not every crime is due to some mental disease, for there are criminals who behave violently though they are in perfect mental health. Otherwise no one will be responsible for any crime!!

5. Fear may also be a cause which leads to violent acts. Fear of the discovery of a crime for example.

A thief may break into a house to steal only, not to murder but they may be forced to do so if anyone sees them for fear of being discovered.

A gang of thieves also may kill some of those who know any secrets concerning them even though they are members of the same gang.

A person may also treat someone violently as a result of thinking that they are plotting against them.

6. Self-conceit and taking pride in strength or misusing power and abilities may also cause violence.

For example, a person beats someone to show that they are more powerful and can overcome them whenever they want. The same thing may be true of some adolescents, some tyrants and some gangs, for they subjugate the members of their gangs to obey their orders.

7. The cause of violence may be wickedness.

A malicious person may give vent to their malice through violence. For example a person may bear ill feelings towards another thinking that they will take their inheritance or their position, so they treat them violently. Jealousy and envy may also lead to the same thing.

The cause may be the wish to repay violence with violence.

8. Misunderstanding may lead to violence.

The Lord Jesus Christ said to His disciples concerning what they were to suffer from the Jews and Romans, *"The time is coming that whoever kills you will think that he offers God service." (Jn. 16:2).*

Due to misunderstanding, some may kill thinking that they abolish the shame of the family or that they are taking revenge.

9. Some may use violence thinking that it is easiest and most immediate solution.

The easiest solution is not always the best. Such persons may see that violence is the only solution and may say, 'Such matters are not to be treated except with violence.' or 'Such a person is not to be treated except with violence'.

10. Violence may also be a kind of craftiness or cunning.

This conforms with the saying, 'Beat the person who is in under your authority and you will be able to control their free will'.

The Holy Bible also says, *"Strike the Shepherd, and the sheep will be scattered..." (Zech. 13:7)*. In this case, violence is not an objective but just a means to the objective.

This leads us to the next cause.

11. Perceived violence.

It is not physical violence. An example is the father who pretends to be angry and threatens to use violence in order to force his son to obey. An employer may threaten to inflict a certain punishment which they do not intend at all to inflect. They do so only to frighten their employees to behave well.

12 Indirect violence.

It is the case of a person who is not in fact violent but uses some violent persons to carry out their purpose instead of them. Here his violence is indirect.

Wrong Violence And Proper Violence

We cannot say that every act of violence is a sin, for there are certain situations which require violence, such as punishing reckless sinners or vile persons or anyone who threatens society with crimes that may destroy it or destroy its traditions and morals.

God Himself mentioned in the Holy Bible some violent punishments which were meant to restrain others and to be a lesson for the next generations because continuous permissiveness may lead to recklessness. Some examples from the Old Testament are the Noah's flood and the event of the earth swallowing Korah, Dothan and Abiram (Num.16). In the New Testament also the example of Ananias and Sapphira is very obvious (Acts 5).

It is said also about a ruler that he does not bear the sword in vain; for he is God's minister, an avenger to execute wrath on him who practices evil (Rom. 13:4,5).

There are certain crimes which if they are not met with violence will be repeated because those who commit them may become reckless and a bad example to others. However, if they are treated firmly and decisively, society will be purified and cleansed.

Here we mention an important spiritual rule:

There is a difference between a public right and a private one. We may be permissive regarding our private rights, out of meekness, love, peace and forgiveness for those who offend us. But we cannot be permissive regarding a public right. We do not possess such a right for it belongs to the whole of society.

Society also needs protection so that the strong may not prevail over the weak.

Thank God